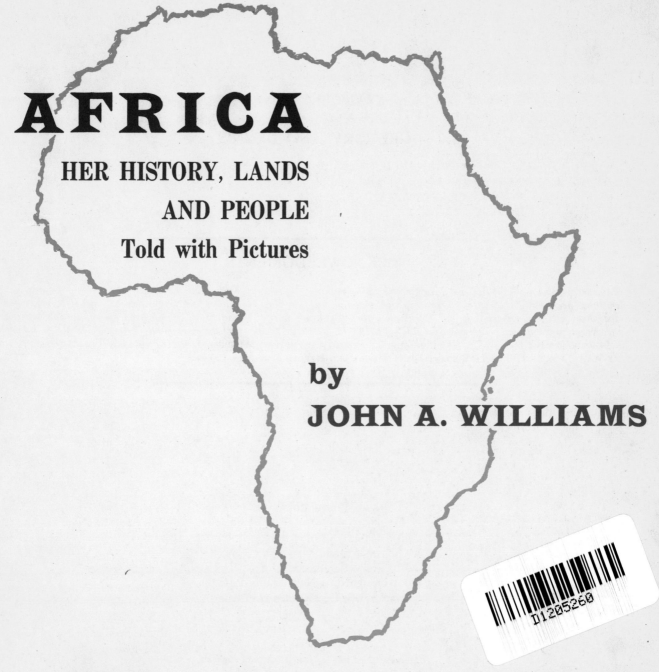

AFRICA

HER HISTORY, LANDS
AND PEOPLE
Told with Pictures

by

JOHN A. WILLIAMS

COOPER
SQUARE
PUBLISHERS, INC. ● NEW YORK, 1962

FOR MY SONS

GREGORY AND DENNIS

ACKNOWLEDGMENTS

One can hardly do a book of this sort — even with its limitations — without researching hundreds of other books and papers which have been written on Africa, not only for material but for corroboration which any work on Africa sorely requires. To list them all would have left but little room for this book itself. Therefore, I acknowledge generally the Africanists of the world, ancient and modern. Specifically, I should like to thank for their valuable assistance and/or comment: JEAN BLACKWELL HUTSON AND THE STAFF OF THE SCHOMBURG COLLECTION, WENDELL J. ROYE, WILLIAM LEO HANSBERRY, JOAN BERRY WAITE, EVA IJAK, BERNICE ROLLINS, ETHEL MINGO, AND HAROLD AND ANN CALIN.

AFRICA:

DOORWAY TO THE PAST

Deep, mysterious and silent, the continent of Africa has been a riddle for ages. She has beckoned for centuries to adventurers, scoundrels, heroes, villains and cowards. All at the same time, Africa is wealth and poverty; beauty and ugliness; hope and despair. Africa is the past and the future; the cradle of life and its graveyard.

Only grudgingly has this paradoxical land surrendered her secrets. In July, 1959, under the merciless sun of Tanganyika at the edge of the Great Rift Valley, the ancient earth yielded up an archaeological treasure.

A scientific expedition, led by Dr. L. S. B. Leakey had for weeks vainly been digging in the sun-baked earth for traces and clues of the earliest man—*Zinjanthropus Boisei*. For many years, anthropologists had believed that East Africa held the remnants of the oldest prehistoric man. But the years of scrabbling, digging and searching had been fruitless until the momentous day in July, 1959, when jubilant scientists returned to their uncomfortable camp and announced that *Zinjanthropus* had been found and another door to the past had been opened.

Zinjanthropus lived among wild sheep, pigs and baboons all of which were much larger then than now. A million seven hundred fifty thousand fascinating years have passed since then and much of Africa has been explored, settled and exploited. Parts of it, however, remain unknown. The great Kalahari Desert, for example, in the southwestern section of the continent, remains in great part a vast, brooding mystery.

When *Zinjanthropus* lived Africa was still being shaped and re-shaped by catastrophic diastrophisms

Bianchi's painting is 1,750,000-year-old Zinjanthropus Boisei.

which formed new mountains and valleys, among them, the Great Rift Valley which runs from Mozambique to the Jordan Valley, 4,000 miles northward. Located along the East African coast, the Great Rift is longer than the United States is wide.

Africa, second only in size to Asia, boasts almost twelve million square miles. She is more than three times the size of continental United States and almost 5,000 miles long. The African coasts run in from the sea and rise to a vast, bountiful plateau in the interior. The northern section of the continent is mostly desert—the Sahara, Libyan and Arabian. Another sandy wasteland is the foreboding Kalahari. Savannas—areas of some vegetation—range southward from the northern deserts to merge with the thick, fierce jungles in Central and West Africa. The weather below the equator is temperate and the seasons are just the opposite of those in Europe and in the United States. Upwards of 236 million people speaking about 800 languages and dialects live in Africa. Her natural resources—gold, uranium, zinc, lead, copper, diamonds, bauxite, petroleum and tin—remain almost untapped. From the tropics come cocoa (more than one half of which is supplied to the world by Africa), cotton, palm products, coffee, rubber and lumber.

This is Africa, vast and with a reserve of wealth that staggers the imagination. She finds herself, with the coming of independence to the vast majority of nations within her boundaries, potentially the most powerful continent in the world.

United Nations

4

SOME FEATURES OF AFRICA

Rivers

Nile	4,160	miles
Congo	2,900	"
Niger	2,600	"
Zambezi	1,600	"
Orange	1,300	"
Senegal	1,050	"
Zimpopo	1,000	"
Gambia	500	"

Lakes

Victoria	26,828	square miles	
Tanganyika	12,700	"	"
Nyasa	11,000	"	"
Rudolf	3,475	"	"
Bangweulu	1,900	"	"
Albert	1,640	"	"
Chad*	7,000	"	"

*In rainy season

Waterfalls

Maletsumyane	630	feet
King Georges	450	"
Victoria	343	"
Aughrabies	Not measured	

Deserts

Sahara	3,500,000	square miles
Kalahari	120,000	" "
Nubian (Sudanese)	Not measured	
Namib (South-West Africa)	Not measured	

Mountain Ranges

Ruwenzori (Mountains of the Moon)	16,000 feet at highest point
Atlas	13,500 " " " "

Highest Peaks

Mt. Kilimanjaro	19,340	feet
Mt. Kenya	17,041	"
Mt. Cameroon	13,500	"

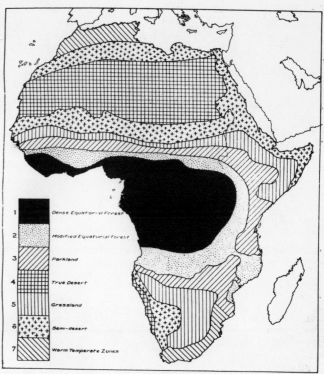

1	Dense Equatorial Forest
2	Modified Equatorial Forest
3	Parkland
4	True Desert
5	Grassland
6	Semi-desert
7	Warm Temperate Zones

United Nations

Climatic and Vegetation Zones

The terrain map on opposite page largely marks the Great Rift Valley along the East African coast ringing the Red Sea. The mountains and deserts in North Africa belie the fact that centuries ago people lived in those regions and, centuries before then, that the ocean filled them. The comparison map below shows the enormous size of Africa.

United Nations

6

Africa, 1961 (opposite page), the year when independence came to more than 20 former colonies. The prehistoric fresco, The White Lady of Brandberg (top), was discovered in South-West Africa in 1917, but the identity of the painter is still unknown. The pyramid at Giza (above) was built during the fourth or Memphite dynasty at the order of Khufu or Cheops. Originally 481 feet high and 750 feet along each side at its base, it took 20 years to build. The sphinx might have been built by another Memphite ruler of the Old Kingdom, Chephren or Khafre, in his own image. Among the ruins of Zimbabwe, an area of 70 acres, is the Acropolis (below). The main temple is oval-shaped and over 200 feet wide, 300 feet long. The Outer Wall is the greatest piece of prehistoric achitecture in Southern Africa. Hebrew slaves (bottom, right) are shown making bricks of mud, straw and stubble in sun-drenched Egypt. The Fulanis of West Africa are believed to be descended from Israelites who fled Egypt before Moses led them to escape.

The Tides of History

Amidst all the uncertainties of Africa, the one certainty is that the limitless Sahara Desert which stretches for more than three million five hundred square miles across North Africa was once habitable as the other deserts must have been. There is ample evidence that at least four separate civilizations flourished in the Sahara from about 4000 B.C. until 2 A.D. There were later empires which came to full fruition during medieval times. Farther south in Nigeria, radio-carbon datings taken from pottery fragments near the village of Nok indicated that a thriving civilization with highly developed art forms flourished as far back as 4000 B.C.

Of the multitudes of findings in Africa, author and historian Basil Davidson said:

"Time and again the achievements of men in Africa—men *of* Africa—have been laid at the door of some mysterious but otherwise unexplained 'people from outside Africa.' It is not only the Hamites who have given scope for the 'inarticulate major premise' of an inherent African (or Negro) inferiority. Over the past fifty years or so, whenever anything remarkable or inexplicable has turned up in Africa, a whole galaxy of non-African (or, at any rate, non-Negro) peoples are dragged in to explain it. The Phoenicians are brought in to explain the Zimbabwe in Rhodesia. The Egyptians are produced as the painters of the 'White Lady' of the Brandberg in South West Africa. Even the Hittites have had their day. Yet every one of those achievements and phenomena is now generally agreed to have had a purely African origin."

(*Lost Cities of Africa*)

While signs of various civilizations appear scattered throughout almost all known Africa, the greatest records of past societies were found around the Nile Valley and even further east. From about 6000 B.C. the peoples who lived in this area—forerunners of the Egyptian and Ethiopian cultures—had a well defined division of labor: jewelers and other craftsmen worked with gold, gems and precious metals; farmers cultivated the fields using plowshares hauled by oxen. There were soldiers

The coming of iron to Africa enabled Egypt, Punt, Kush and Axum to effect a transition from the Bronze to the Iron Age. Ethiopia was one of the first nations to profit by this. Notice the hand and foot bellows and the kiln.

Rameses the Great (1301-1234 B.C.) (above), had one of the longest reigns in Egyptian history. Occupied in a long war with the Hittites (1272) which involved the historic battle at Kadesh, Rameses triumphed and spent the rest of his life on a building program. Rameses is believed to have been the Pharaoh at the time of the Exodus. Among the most important Pharaohs of the New Kingdom dynasties were (below) Thothmes III (1500-1445 B.C.) called the "Alexander the Great" of Egypt, and Amenhotep III, his great grandson (1411-1375 B.C.), a patron of the arts. Both were Kushites from the area which is now the Sudan. Thothmes led his armies to 17 victories; 17 of his 32-years' rule were spent in battle. He lived at ancient Thebes on the Nile. Ethiopian and Egyptian Queens are shown bottom right. Ethiopia, Punt and Kush were often confused and given the same name—Ethiopia. The queens of Kush for quite some time held all power of the thrones and were buried in pyramids somewhat smaller than those in Egypt; ruins are still found at Meroë.

and tradesmen; mechanics and laborers; rulers and ruled.

The Egyptians, influenced by invaders from the South and East, had a long and momentous history. During those periods when Egypt was strong enough to beat back her enemies, the Pharaohs or kings had built one of the most remarkable engineering and architectural feats of all history—the Pyramids—which were erected as tomb-monuments to the Pharaohs.

The first Pyramid was constructed at Giza by the Pharaoh Cheops (2900-2877 B.C.). The Pyramid of Cheops still stands and is regarded as one of the world's great wonders.

Almost from the outset much of the power and wealth of Egypt came as a result of contacts with the civilizations which lay south of her: Meroè, Ethiopia or Kush, Nubia—now known as the Sudan, and Punt—now called Somaliland. For an interminable length of time

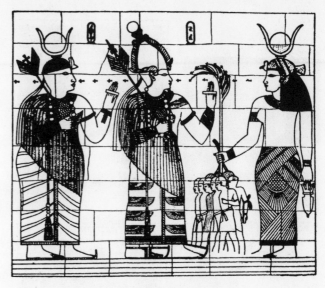

The above battle was between Tahraka, king of Ethiopia, and Shabatok, king of Egypt, in 692 B.C. Bas relief (right) believed by Prof. Hansberry to be of King Neketamen and Queen Amentere who reigned over Western Ethiopia at the birth of Christ. Ptoleman map (below, left) shows the unsuccessful voyage of Hanno (475 B.C.) of Carthage to Cape Palmas with 60 ships and 30,000 men and women. Ancient map (bottom, right) marks the earliest known world with its division of people and the Ocean River theory.

armies from these countries marched north to battle with the Egyptians; Egypt on the other hand, sent her armies out on conquering missions.

Stationed as she was at the head of the Mediterranean Sea and at the curve leading into Asia Minor, Egypt was constantly open to invasions by Babylonian, Persian, Arabian, Hittite, Greek and Roman armies, each of which left some mark on her culture.

Warfare flared in and around Egypt for centuries. From time to time, one power then another was dominant but by 575 B.C. Ethiopia emerged as the greatest nation of the world. Iron, which had been discovered in Asia Minor, came to Africa about 600 B.C. and the Ethiopians used it to forge weapons of war which enabled them to hold Egypt as a colony for more than one hundred years. This was possible because the greatest iron smelting centers were controlled by the Ethiopians in their captured provinces.

With most of the activity going on in the northeast corner of Africa it is not difficult to understand why the great bulk of Africa remained unexplored. Some information did trickle back. Thales, a Greek philosopher (610-540 B.C.), was one of the first mapmakers to base his maps on information received from explorers, rumors and wild guesswork. Thales advanced the "Ocean River Theory" which assumed that a great river, filled with hideous, howling monsters that could swallow a ship at a single gulp, flowed through the center of Africa from east to west.

Beyond this river which none could traverse, there lay other lands, according to Thales. As late as the fifteenth century, this fantasy still had adherents though many adventurers, especially the Portuguese, had crossed the "raging" river unharmed. Thales's river was the Niger which some confused with the Congo, further to the south.

Sporadic efforts at exploring Africa were undertaken. The first major effort was made by the Carthaginians in 530 B.C. and settlements were established around Cape Palmas along the bulge of West Africa. But events of momentous proportions changed the base of power in Africa during the fourth century B.C. when Alexander of Macedonia vanquished Egypt. The young conqueror might well have become the ruler of the world but contracted a fatal illness and died in Babylon (323 B.C.) at the age of thirty-three.

Next followed the sparkling reign of the Ptolemies who ruled from 323 B.C. to 30 B.C. Cleopatra was the last of the Ptolemy line and was defeated at Actium in 31 B.C. by the Romans who had brought about not only Egypt's downfall, but that of Carthage as well. Carthage, now the modern city of Tunis, was razed by the Roman General Scipio Africanus after the Battle of Zama in 202 B.C.

By now the Roman Empire was an established institution. It lasted from 27 B.C. to 476 A.D., attaining its peak in 180 A.D. The impact of the Romans on North Africa, on all the world, is indelible. To this day, roads, aqueducts and walls built by the Romans are still in use in Africa as well as in Europe.

About the time of Christ (25 A.D.), trade between China and the Red Sea nations took place; it would continue well into the thirteenth century, the Chinese employing ships greater in size and better in performance than any sailing ship devised by a European nation at that time.

Indonesians came too, sailing great outrigger canoes and following the stars. Some types of outrigger canoes are still being used in East Africa and Madagascar, now the Malagasy Republic.

Pictured above (left) is Alexander the Great. Cleopatra (above, right) is seen from a wall of the Temple of Denderah in Upper Egypt. The formidable ships of the Roman navy (as below) transported troops, swept pirates clear of the sealanes and shipped valuable produce from the provinces back to Rome. To the left are the prows of a bireme and a trireme, fighting ships with ramming devices; to the right are the aft sections of a bireme and trireme—the former housed two banks of slaves who pulled oars and the latter three banks. In the center is a three-masted trireme. On the opposite page (top, left) are Publius Cornelius Scipio "Africanus" and Hannibal (medallion), leader of the Carthaginians who was defeated at Zama by Scipio Africanus.

During the Middle Ages, which started with the collapse of the Roman Empire, as tumultuous change occurred in Europe Africa too was embroiled in a cycle of great changes. The known world, released so suddenly from the cultured but firm grip of Rome, drifted without will or direction until the advent of Mohammed, the founder of Islam.

Mohammed, a camel driver, was born in Arabia about 570 A.D. He died sixty-two years later. The religion he founded, which relied heavily on the Old Testament, now has some one hundred million converts in Africa. Christianity in Africa has forty-five million and in the middle are some eighty million "pagans." There are five million Coptic Christians. The Crusades (1096-1244) and later penetrations during the fourteenth, fifteenth and successive centuries did much to break down tribal customs and religions. Today, as European nations withdraw, leaving something of a religious vacuum, more and more Africans are turning to Mohammedanism.

What brought the Europeans into the Holy Land was the Arab invasion of Africa about 600 A.D. and later in the eleventh century. The Arabs spread completely across the top of Africa, and plunged southward into the Sudan. They tried to enter Europe from Constantinople but had failed. Now the far western forces of the Arabian armies reached across Gibraltar, where in the dawn of time a land bridge had existed, and invaded the Iberian peninsula in 711 A.D. By 732 they had marched into France as they sought to conquer all of Europe. They were stopped at Tours by Charles Martel, known as "The Hammer." The invaders, known variously as Moors, Berbers or Saracens, were rolled back to Spain and Portugal and finally expelled from Europe

Typical of the Roman ruins in North Africa are these (top) in the market-place of the Roman colony of Thamugadi. Centuries ago Indonesians came to Africa sailing outrigger canoes (of which the above is a small version) designed to hold 20 men Below is a modification of a Chinese ship; their greatest vessels had five decks and four to seven masts.

11

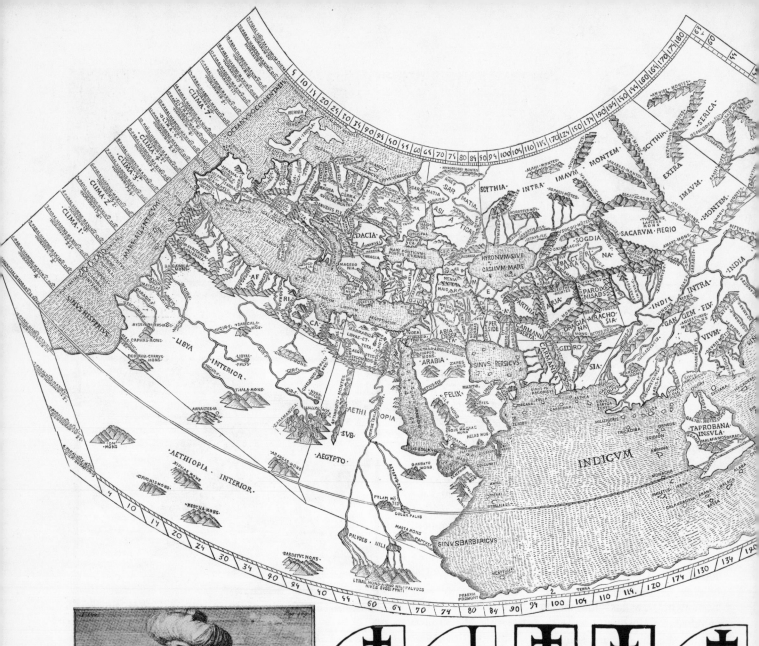

MAHOMETH

12

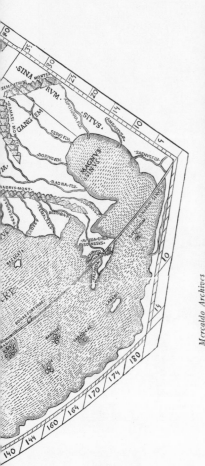

Mercaldo Archives

Opposite page: *The mystery of Africa is clearly obvious in this Ptolemy map (top) of about 160 A.D. The print (extreme left) is an early European conception of Mohammed. He began teaching in 610; tribal leaders opposed his beliefs and in 620 chased him from Mecca to Medina. This journey is called the Year of the Flight, or the Hejira and is celebrated by Moslems all over the world. The flags (center) represent the Coptic kingdoms of the 14th century; Ethiopia today is mostly Coptic. Charles Martel, The Hammer, is shown in battle (bottom). Like the Alhambra (above), the jewel box (left) carved from ivory in the 10th century was a product of Moorish artists. The Alhambra still stands as a tribute to the Moorish kings of the 1300s. Godfrey, Raymond, Tancred and Bohemond, 4 noblemen (below), led the First Crusade to the Holy Land in 1096 and brought Europeans contact with rich African cultures.*

in 1492. They had brought a civilization and an architecture to Europe, however, which has never been equalled. The Alhambra, palace of the Moorish kings completed in Granada, Spain, in the fourteenth century, is a primary example. The Moors also laced the dry country with irrigation canals which brought new prosperity to the country. Centuries later the Spanish filled in these canals and the land rapidly returned to its former arid state.

From the East the Chinese continued their voyages to the African continent. It is believed that the mariner's compass was first used by them, coming into use by European sailors long after the eleventh century.

A recent theory discloses that Arabs from port Dar-el-Beida (Casablanca, Morocco) sailing about 1100 A.D. "due west for full an hundred days . . . in ships as wide as clouds" discovered "Mu-lan-p'i" or the northern tip of South America. This theory, advanced by Dr. Hui-Lin-Li of the American Oriental Society, traced native African foods into the new world. Some of these were: corn, pumpkin, avocado, guava, papaya and pineapple. The Chinese, however, were the only people known to have had vessels whose sails might have approached the description, "wide as clouds."

THE GIANT STIRS

The famous Catalan map (above) of Jewish cartographer, Abraham Cresques, the most detailed and accurate of its time, was completed in 1375 at the Jewish Cartographer's School, Majorca, Spain. Legendary Timbuktu (top, opposite) page) was first mentioned by Herodotus in the 5th century. Before the arrival of the Arabs in the 6th century, Timbuktu, a trade center and university city which lay in the Songhay Empire, was purely Negro. Later, Arabs, Jews and Negroes worked, taught and studied without restriction together. At the extreme right is a Benin statue. Abu Abdallah Mohammed ibn-Batuta (1304-1377) might have looked like this (right) in his role as the greatest Arabian traveler of the Middle Ages. Shown is bactrian, a 2-humped camel.

As Europe blossomed and flourished during the golden years of its Renaissance and the best of western culture came to full flower, Africa was also enjoying a Golden Age of Enlightenment. And as the European Renaissance had been influenced by outside forces such as Marco Polo's contact with the Chinese so was the African Renaissance similarly influenced by the events in Europe. There had been some contact between Africa and Europe for many centuries across the nine-mile span of water that separated North Africa from Gibraltar.

Thus, one growing culture affected another. As Europe grew and spread, as knowledge and art filtered across the boundaries of distance, feeding itself into Africa, so did African intellectualism drift back to Europe. Arabic numerals, for example, came to Europe about the twelfth century.

Africa was the seat of much culture and education; there were universities, medical schools and law schools. One of the greatest centers was Timbuktu. Leo Africanus in *Descriptions of Africa* (1550) said:

"... at Timbuktu sit numerous judges, doctors and clerics all appointed by the king. He greatly honors men of learning. More profit is made from the book trade than from all other branches of commerce."

Africanus was an Arab traveler and geographer who, captured by pirates and sent as a slave to Rome, became a linguist and writer.

Timbuktu can still be found on present day maps as Timbuctoo—it is in the Mali Republic and was but one of the famed university cities in Africa. It reached its greatest period under Askias Mohammed I, "The Great" (1493-1528). Other great university cities were at Soukore, Gao, Walata and Djenné. The Medieval University of West Africa was located within the boundaries of the Songhai Empire. Another culture was that of the Bournou which lasted from 1000 to 1645 A.D.

Under Askias, religious tolerance spread throughout that part of Africa which came under the influence of the universities. Jew, Christian and Mohammedan alike studied laws on banking, commerce and credit set down by the king. The study of the arts and sciences was also pursued.

In addition, there also flourished the highly regarded Mali Empire which, under King Sundiata Keita (1230-1255), expanded by capturing the kingdoms of Ghana and Gambia in 1235 and then consolidating and enriching all provinces during the reign of King Kanka Musa (1307-1332).

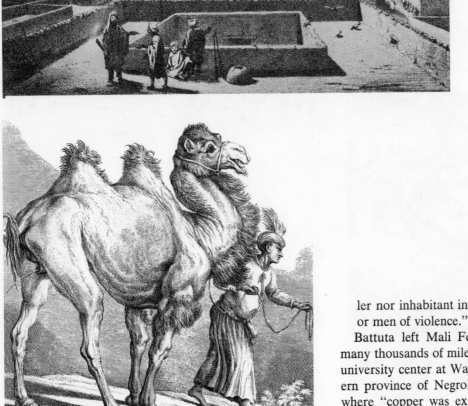

Ibn Battuta (1304-1369) a native of Tangier and one of the foremost chroniclers of medieval Africa wrote of the Mali Kingdom in which he arrived June 28, 1352:

"I was at Mali during the two festivals of the sacrifice and the fast-breaking. On these days the sultan takes his seat on the pempi after the mid-afternoon prayer. The armour-bearers bring in magnificent arms—quivers of gold and silver, swords ornamented with gold and golden scabbards, gold and silver lances and crystal araces. At his hand stand four emirs driving off flies, having in their hands silver ornaments resembling saddle-stirrups . . . .

"The Negroes are seldom unjust and have a greater abhorrence of injustice than any other people. Their sultan shows no mercy to anyone who is guilty of the least act of it. There is complete security in their country. Neither travel-

ler nor inhabitant in it has any fear from robbers or men of violence."

Battuta left Mali February 27, 1353. He covered many thousands of miles in Africa and Asia, visiting the university center at Walata, which he called the "northern province of Negroland," and Tagadda (Takedda) where "copper was exported to the town of Kubar in the regions of the heathens and to Zaghara and to the country of Bournu, which is forty days' journey from Tagadda." Both Zaghara and Bournu would today be near the western border of the Mali Republic.

Not only Battuta, but other travelers were visiting Africa. South and east along the coast, the Chinese were plying the waters with ships up to five decks high and with four to seven masts. As early as 600 A.D. the brilliant naval architect, Yang Su, was primarily responsible for designing these large ships which boasted water-tight bulkheads, stern rudders and spinning sails to keep the vessels headed into the wind. Yang Su was far ahead of his time; it was not until the fifteenth century that Europeans learned the art of sailing three-masters. Under the Sung Dynasties (906-1279) Chinese maritime trade reached an all-time high.

Pushing inland from the ancient port of Sofala in Mozambique, the Chinese and perhaps Indian and Indonesian sailors probably had some contact with the Zimbabwe civilization in Rhodesia, and may even have established some relationship with the Mapungubwe, who worked in gold. One of the greatest mysteries in

SOFALA

Magical Sofala (above), now Beira in Mozambique, was a port city for the Portuguese, Dutch and British trade; it is shown here as an early Portuguese colony. Medieval armor (see African warrior below) is still used by soldiers of the Lake Chad region for important occasions.

This map drawn by Professor William Leo Hansberry marks the principle kingdoms, cities and towns of Africa during the Middle Ages from the Red Sea to the Atlantic. Spellings have altered; "Melle," for example, is now Mali.

history is why the Chinese, who opened the doors to large-craft sailing, suddenly recalled their vessels from the seas and destroyed both ships and ports.

In the north, Kanka Musa in 1325 took over the Songhai capital of Gao and then brought all of Mali under his domination. It was during Kanka Musa's time that Ibn Battuta saw the wealth of the empire which also included the great salt deposits at Taghaza on the northern edge of the Sahara, the approaches to the gold country to the south and the copper country at Tagadda.

The reports of such men as Battuta, the whispers, rumors and tales about Africa that sifted through to Europe, awakened an interest in that continent. There was concrete evidence—gold, jewelry and spices—which showed that Africa was rich; many men thought of it as the gateway to India, which was mistakenly believed to be located in the lower half of Africa.

The effect of all these cumulative bits and pieces was an increasing drive to learn more about Africa. This movement was given added impetus with the spread of the Ottoman Empire (1300-1922). When the island of Majorca was occupied by the Turks, a Jewish mapmaker, Abraham Cresques, produced in 1375 the so-called "Catalan Map" of North Africa. This map did for North Africa what Columbus did for the New World; it opened the way for a flood of exploration of Africa by Europeans of various nationalities. Its mysteries were about to be probed seriously for the first time—the Age of Exploration was at hand for Africa.

THE OPENING DOOR

Prince Henry, "The Navigator," son of King John I of Portugal, had grand ambitions for his country; probably the grandest was his desire to see Portugal as the greatest and richest power in the world. He had fought in North Africa at the battle of Ceuta, Morocco, in 1415, and had become fascinated with Africa; he felt that somehow Portugal's future lay in that vast land and was himself fired with curiosity about the unknown parts of it. He resolved to secure those lands and whatever riches they might hold for his country.

Under Prince Henry's guidance, the first well-organized European explorations began about 1434. Prince Henry personally accompanied several expeditions which penetrated beyond the desert and into the fringes of West Africa. All through the mid-fifteenth century, Portuguese mariners poked along the coastline of Africa. The purpose of these expeditions was twofold. In addition to claiming African territory and monopolizing what treasures might be found—gold, gems spices, silks—Prince Henry was also seeking a short cut to India which was the goal of every European mercantile nation. (It was while searching for such a route that Columbus discovered the New World.) Doggedly pursuing these aims, the hardy Portuguese sea captains pushed into the unknown, along Africa's northwest coast. Cape Bojador was rounded by Gil Eanes in 1434; eleven years later, Dinis Dias discovered Cape Verde. By 1480, the entire Guinea coastline had been explored.

Slowly, patiently and expertly, the Portuguese extended their voyages. In 1488, Captain Bartolomeu Dias rounded the Cape of Good Hope and ten years later Vasco da Gama, one of the greatest Portuguese explorers, not only went around the Cape but sailed up Africa's east coast, touched at several points and went on to India. Pedro Alvares Cabral (1460-1526) in attempting to duplicate this feat was blown far off course and was carried to Brazil (April, 1500). He finally rounded the Cape of Good Hope and established a base in India.

Portugal claimed sovereignty over all the places her navigators had discovered. Numerous forts and trading posts were set up along the Guinea Coast; the first of these in 1482 at San Jorge da Mina. The shrewd Portuguese began to exploit the rich territory even as the explorations continued. They found gold, ivory, spices

Pictured, top to bottom, are Prince Henry, a Portuguese ship, Diaz, da Gama, and Cabral. Prince Henry "The Navigator" (1394-1460) made no voyages himself but improved the compass and methods of shipbuilding. Ship is of the Portuguese navy, 15th century. Bartolomeu Diaz (1450?-1500) was the first Portuguese captain to open the route to India when he rounded the Cape of Good Hope in 1488. Admiral Vasco da Gama (1469-1524) settled colonies at Malindi, Sofala and Mozambique on the Africa east coast in 1502. Pedro Alvares Cabral (1460-1526), enroute to India, was blown to Brazil which he claimed for Portugal. He rounded the Cape of Good Hope and went on to Calcutta.

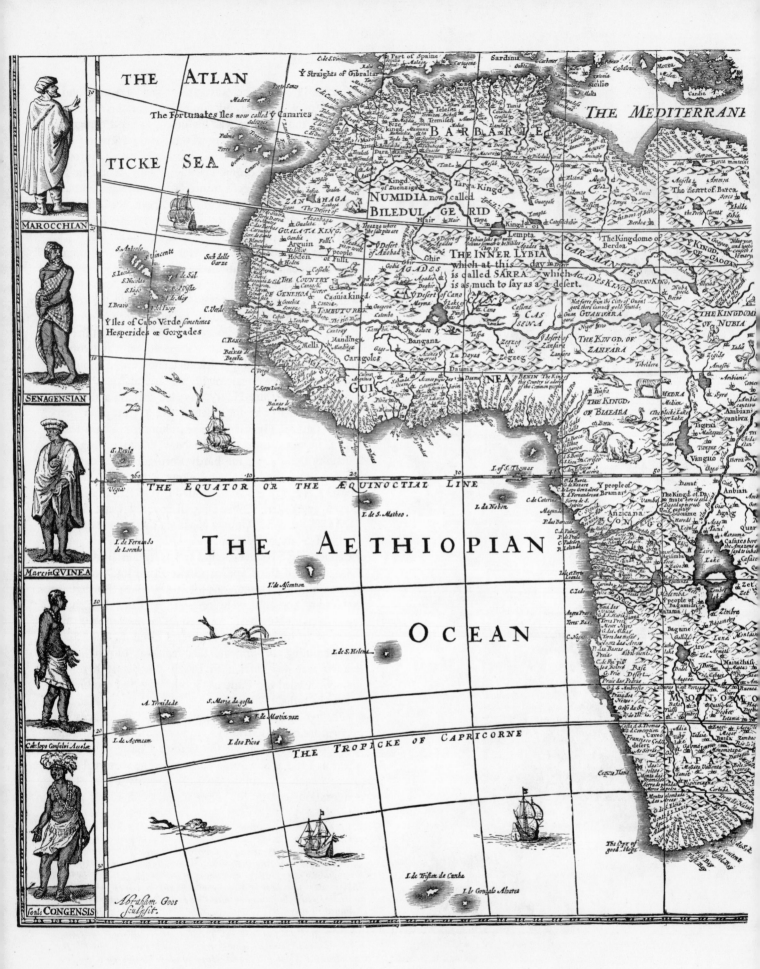

NATOLIA
Cyprus
...AN SEA
PART OF ASIA

AFRICÆ, described the manners of their Habits, and buildinge: newly done into English by I.S and published at the charges of G. Humble Ano 1626

ÆGYPT

ARABIA

Y ARABIAN

AND THE

INDIAN SEA

THE o BARBA:

RIAN GULFE

MADAGASCAR, which is also called S. LAURENCE ILAND

THE EAST OCEAN

EGYPTIAN

ABISSINIAN

MOZAMBIQUEAN

MADAGASCAR

habit of cape of goodhope

This 1626 map shows that the Ocean River theory had been discarded. As a whole it is fairly accurate. The interior, however, shows still a great deal of error and fancy. Note the peoples of various lands and the flying fish and sea monsters. Above is Admiral da Gama's flagship, the São Gabriel which the Portuguese sailor used on his voyages. From its log came this description of the people of an East African port: "two senhores of the country came to see us. They were very haughty and valued nothing we gave them . . . A young man in their company . . . had come from a distant country and had already seen big ships like ours." The ships he had seen were probably Chinese.

traders managed to get in silk, cotton, grain, ivory and gold. By 1525 the Portuguese had to push inland to seek out the wealth the Africans and Arabs refused to give them or had hidden from them; they had to push beyond the Caffre (Kaffir), Hottentot and Monomotapa tribal territories which overlapped.

On the west coast the Portuguese, unable to derive as much gold from the Africans as they'd wished, intensified slave traffic. Under the pretense of saving the souls of the captives, they shipped them to Portugal.

The tides of history turned slowly against Portugal as other nations went into ascendancy in Africa. In the seventeenth century, it passed finally from Portugal to Holland and from Holland in the eighteenth and nineteenth centuries to France and England. Later, Italy, Spain, Germany and Belgium managed to get their shares of the African spoils.

These animals were found by early explorers in Ethiopia and Kenya. Their imaginations were vivid—note the heavy-tailed sheep wheeling his appendage on a wagon. The sea horse was the hippopotamus, the fig tree was a banana tree.

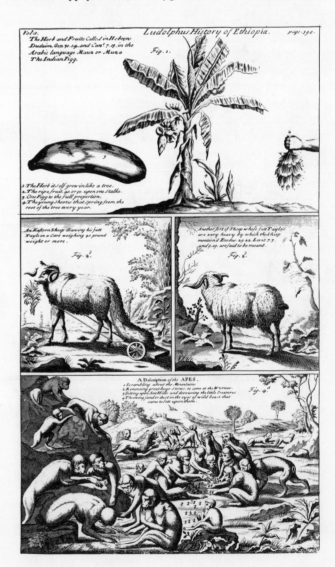

and another commodity for which the demand began to rise—slaves.

This trade in human beings became the most lucrative of all Africa's riches; before the advent of the Portuguese, the slave trade had been comparatively small and confined to the areas of Northern Africa. By the mid-sixteenth century, Portugal's monopoly on Africa's wealth—human and mineral—was being seriously challenged by the English, Danish, Swedish and Dutch.

The period of the greatest explorations approaching its end, the Portuguese settled down to consolidate their finds and to ship the wealth of Africa back to Lisbon. The presence of the Portuguese on the East African coast cut off trade with India, the Indians having already experienced Portuguese warfare with da Gama and other aggressive visitors. Sofala was established as the Portuguese base of operations in plundering nearby cities and the interior. But the gold they sought was taken from the first in disappointingly small quantities.

Trade in cloth fell off. The *zambucos,* ships from the northern coast and from India, sometimes came but more often did not. Smuggling took place and the Arab

A CONTINENT IN CHAINS

"**A** Dutch man of warre that sold us twenty Negars . . ."

So wrote the Englishman, John Rolfe, as he watched a ship hove to off Jamestown, Virginia, in the year 1619. Aboard that Dutch vessel were twenty Senegalese natives; with their sale to the English colonists of Jamestown, Negro slavery was introduced into the New World. No man then could foresee that a business transaction involving a score of African tribesmen would touch off the great American Civil War over two hundred years later, or that deep problems of social and political equality stemming from the introduction of slavery would still be plaguing the United States after more than three centuries.

The Portuguese and the Dutch made a rich business of selling Africans into slavery; but the English, who had come into Africa on the heels of the Portuguese, became the most prolific slavers in modern history.

In 1562 an Englishman, Sir John Hawkins, who later was to win fame as a naval commander, took one hundred men in three ships and "partly by sword and partly by other means" captured three hundred Africans in North-West Africa and carried them straightway to the Spanish islands of the west.

The Dutch and British, their forts within firing range of each other along the Gold Coast (Ghana), plied their trade in slaves under the auspices of the Dutch East India Company and the British Royal African Company.

The latter eventually "gave" Britain a complete slave monopoly from Morocco to the Cape of Good Hope. British slave trade was to last 271 years before it was abolished.

While the British raided for slaves, their explorations did not begin in force until the nineteenth century after which they moved to "protect" and finally colonize great sections of the continent. By then Portugal had exhausted her strength and finance and was no longer able to hold on to the territory she had colonized. However, she still holds sizeable portions of Africa including Mozambique, Portuguese Guinea, São Tomé, the Cape Verde Islands and Angola.

When the British came they chose and staked out their lands, as had the slavers and colonizers before them, with utter disregard for ancient tribal boundaries, languages, customs and dialects.

Human beings became Africa's most valuable commodity for trade. Before slavery was abolished in the

The Era of Slavery

Slaves captured in ancient wars were the property of the community, such as these Negro slaves (top) whose capture was depicted on the Egyptian monuments at ancient Thebes. Antam Gonsalves, a Portuguese raider, brought the first black slaves to Portugal in 1443. The chronicler, Azurara, said, however, that "amongst them were some white enough, fair to look upon and well proportioned, others were less white . . . and others again were so black as Ethiops." Christopher Columbus is shown greeting the Indians of Hispanola he enslaved (above). So ferocious were the Spanish slavemasters that the Indians began to die out and African slaves were then imported to the New World by the thousands.

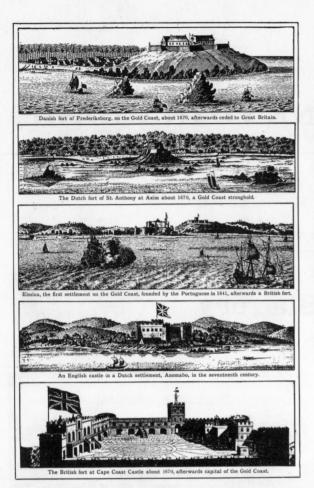

Danish fort of Frederiksborg, on the Gold Coast, about 1670, afterwards ceded to Great Britain.

The Dutch fort of St. Anthony at Axim about 1670, a Gold Coast stronghold.

Elmina, the first settlement on the Gold Coast, founded by the Portuguese in 1841, afterwards a British fort.

An English castle in a Dutch settlement, Anomabo, in the seventeenth century.

The British fort at Cape Coast Castle about 1670, afterwards capital of the Gold Coast.

At left are forts of European powers in Africa that carried on slave trading during the 17th century. In the space of only 20 years the British shipped a third of a million slaves from Cape Coast Castle. A Royal African (or Guinea) Company official treaty-making with the chiefs of the Gold Coast in 1672 (above). The treaties gave the RAC more land to raid for slaves. Slave raids (below) upon African villages were secret, swift and murderous.

United States by the thirteenth amendment in 1865, slave raids and the tortuous voyages across the Atlantic "Middle Passage" had killed twenty to thirty-five million unfortunate Africans—a genocide unmatched in all history. Though six to twelve million may have arrived in the Americas, in 1850 there were just slightly more than three million slaves in the United States.

From the earliest times slaves had been the bauble in the crown of a king or chief or sultan or pharaoh. Slaves belonged to the community which had enslaved them, not to a single master.

The pharaohs could build great temples and pyramids at no cost to the citizens by using slaves; the Spartans could involve themselves in numerous wars and be assured that when they returned home whatever crops could be sown on the rocky land would be harvested by slaves. Deep in the African interior, dying empires flickered and tried to persist with foundations of slaves captured in the interminable intra-tribal wars.

With the coming of the Roman Empire slavery moved slowly but surely into the hands not of the public but of the individual. Ostentatious displays of great numbers of slaves, the shift of the Roman farmer to the cities, the land shrinking under the vast numbers of conquered peoples who soon began to outnumber the Romans, all contributed to the birth of the proverb, "so many slaves—so many foes." Few races of people have escaped slavery; it has always been a human condition.

As bad as slavery had been in the Orient, in Africa, in Europe—anywhere in the world—nothing like it existed until Europeans began plundering the African coasts for human beings who had become more valuable than the gold they possessed. African chiefs, sometimes working with Arab slave traders, also aided this traffic for a time. No people had been so completely sheared from a past as the black African; no people had been shunted so far from home; no people had been so utterly unable to communicate with the master who had captured him.

The lines of the distribution of slaves into the Americas blurred quickly, but in the beginning Portuguese and British raiders preyed along the Grain or Ivory Coasts of the western bulge of Africa enslaving Mandingo, Fulani and Jolof tribesmen. These were sent to the Spanish islands in Central America.

Later, joined by the Dutch and the Danes, the slavers captured Ashanti, Fanti, Akan (all sometimes labelled Coromantes) and in rare cases, Hausa, from what are now Ghana, Nigerian and Dahomean coasts. These went to the British West Indies.

In the last of the eighteenth and the beginning of the nineteenth century, however, slave traders had more and more contact with the Portuguese who held most of the ports in the Congo. Cabinda, a Portuguese enclave at the mouth of the Congo, was one of the most

This slave market (top) stood on the island of Zanzibar. Merchants from Arabia and parts of Africa gathered here to buy slaves and take them to their various homes. The British, although determined to stamp out this slave trade, could not. These were the types of vessels (above) used to carry slaves from the mainland to Zanzibar. Lt. V. L. Cameron of the Royal Navy (1844-1884) in exploring Africa sketched a slave gang (below) being led from Central Africa to the coast in 1876—years after slavery had been outlawed by almost every European nation and America. Illegal slave trade flourished off East African coast as Arabs continued to raid and enslave. Cut-away drawing shows slave quarters aboard a Zanzibar slaver. 30,000 were exported annually to Arabia in the 1870's.

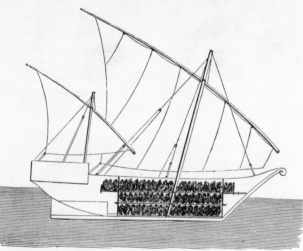

Slavers (top) run a human cargo along the east coast of Africa. Diagram above and picture below show method of packing slaves under the hatches of a ship which also carried cargo. Journey from African west coast to South America, depending upon the weather, took an average of a month and a half. Cholera, dysentery, smallpox and a host of other diseases often rendered a whole ship helpless. When chased by British warships after the British had abolished slavery, crews threw slaves, still in chains, into the sea in order not to be caught with the evidence. Implements of slave torture (above, right) were fiendish. Tuareg slave hunters (below, right) were often hired by Arabs or European traders to capture hapless villagers. Chiefs of villages often sold their people to the raiders.

SHIPMENTS OF SLAVES INTO SOUTH CAROLINA FOR THE YEARS 1710 TO 1796:		
Source of origin given as "Africa"		20,564
Gambia (including Senegal and Goree)		3,652
"Guinea" (from sources indicated as Gold Coast, Cabocorso Castle, Bande, Bance Island and Windward Coast)		6,777
Calabar (Old Calabar, New Calabar and Bonny)		9,224
Angola		3,860
Madagascar		1,011
Slaves brought directly from Africa	45,088	
Slaves imported from the West Indies	7,046	
Slaves imported from other American ports	370	
		52,504
1733-1785:		
Origin as "Africa"		4,146
The Gambia to Sierra Leone		12,441
Sierra Leone		3,906
Liberia and the Ivory Coast (Rice and Grain Coasts)		3,851
Guinea Coast (Gold Coast to Calabar)		18,240
Angola		11,485
Congo		10,924
Mozambique		243
East Africa		230
Imported from Africa	65,466	
Imported from the West Indies	2,303	
		67,769

notorious ports through which the Portuguese and other slavers passed out their human cargo. The tribespeople who lived here, near the mouth of the Congo River, were Bateke, Babembe, Bakongo, Bayaka and Basuku among many others, and were generally delivered to the nearest American port, Brazil.

Slave holders had certain preferences among the tribes. The French preferred Dahomeans (Whydahs, Paw Paws or Po Pos). The British preferred slaves from the Gold Coast except the Ibo from Nigeria who were believed inclined toward suicide as a result of punishment. The Ashanti and Fanti became rebellious under punishment. The Yorubas (Nagot) were considered fine slaves because of their apparent meekness.

All heroes and great men have more than one side; this was true of Christopher Columbus who was directly responsible for beginning chattel slavery in the Americas (Haiti) before the start of the sixteenth century. Columbus dealt in Indians who were cruelly oppressed by the Spanish.

Bartolomé de Las Casas was a missionary who saw the Indians dying from overwork; work to which they were not accustomed. Las Casas went to his superior, Cardinal Ximenes, and pleaded that the Indians be replaced with the hardier Africans. By now the Indians were not only dying from overwork, they were dying out as a race. The African, Las Casas and others argued, was robust and virile and capable of doing, each one, the work of more than four Indians.

Ximenes wrestled with the problem; after all, being under Spanish domination the Indian could more easily be converted to the Faith. But Ximenes reasoned with remarkable foresight that, since Africans were a strong and durable race, in Haiti they would breed fast (as they did in their native land) and before long, numbering more than the Spanish, would rebel and the island would be rent with revolutions.

While the authorities argued pro and con about the Africans and the Indians, Isabella and then Ferdinand died and the throne was assumed by Charles V, seventeen years old. Charles gave his favorite subjects, ignoring the failing Ximenes's advice, settlements in Haiti, Cuba, Jamaica and Puerto Rico and made arrangements to supply these territories with 4,000 African slaves a year. Slavery had come in force to the Americas.

However, neither in England nor America did slavery go unopposed. The very concept of human beings treated as chattel sickened many decent men, and strong abolitionist movements stirred in both countries. Slavery in the British Isles was terminated June 22, 1772, and in the British Empire in 1833. Although England had been the greatest supplier of slaves, the abhorrence of the practice aroused great protest against it.

The British abolitionists were led by Granville Sharpe (1735-1813), an English philanthropist zealous in the cause of liberation of the slaves. He communicated with an American Quaker, Anthony Benezet, and both fought for legislation which culminated in the British actions. American Quakers from the beginning had forbidden members to own slaves. The American Congress of 1774 attempted to outlaw slave trading and transportation, but the law was not enforced. Slavery in the United States was finally ended by the adoption of the thirteenth amendment in 1865. However, long before this, when individual states attempted to enforce the law of 1774, slave breeding took place and became foremost of the many ugly and vicious aspects of slavery which existed in the United States.

As a result of pressures from Quakers and abolitionists the British, in 1807, when it had made slavery illegal but was unable to really enforce this edict, established the Colony and Protectorate of Sierra Leone for repatriated slaves and honorably discharged African servicemen. Similar pressures in America had resulted in the birth of Liberia in 1822. It was a haven for slaves who had been returned to Africa. Liberia, whose capital city was named Monrovia in honor of the American president, became the first African Republic in 1847.

Granville Sharp became a British Abolitionist after infamous "Zong Affair" in which slaves were drowned at sea.

Sometimes anti-slavery patrols or missionaries were able to halt the abduction of slaves from Africa, as seen above.

Slaves captured in raids were examined for fitness and hardiness (above). Depletion of Africans by slavers destroyed customs, cultures and mores to such an extent that Africa still has not recovered from its effects. This drawing (below) reveals the parting of mother and daughter, and a child at the breast of its mother. When the slave trade was drawing to a close, slave breeding became the method by which more slaves were propagated.

The Slaves Strike Back

Mercaldo Archives

Historians have sometimes ignored the efforts of slaves to regain their freedom. There is scant mention of the often heroic measures taken by the enslaved Africans to break away from their masters. A look at the record of slave rebellions shatters the myth of Negro docility under the yoke of bondage in the Caribbean, South America and the United States.

The truth is that slavery in the western hemisphere caused more than 250 known revolts—some of chilling ferocity—beginning with uprisings in Haiti in 1522. Eleven rebellions alone took place before the end of the next year. A remarkable revolt occurred in the province of Pernambuco, Brazil, where slaves breaking away set up the Republic of Palmares, named after its great forest of palm trees. They raided neighboring villages for women and fielded a fighting force of some 30,000 men. They flourished for sixty-seven years. Eventually, the Portuguese with 7,000 men and artillery surrounded the capital and crushed this former, Brazilian, Negro slave society.

The "Black Republic" (1797) set up in Haiti by Toussaint Louverture (1743-1803) during the slavery period was but another of the many examples of slave rebellions. New York, called New Netherlands in the 1700's had an uprising in 1712. By 1775 there were over 2,456 African slaves in the region now encompassed by Greater New York.

Quaco, a leader of a slave revolt ("The Great Negro Plot") was burned at the stake in New York in 1741. Four whites were hung and fourteen other Negroes were burned for planning the massacre of all whites in the city. The year of the American revolution, another plot was discovered and squelched. This one was to have combined the forces of Indian and Negro slaves against the city.

But the greatest revolts were led by a slave named Gabriel (1800) and Nat Turner (1831), both in Virginia, and one by Denmark Vesey in South Carolina in 1822. The effect of the rebellions was swift. Alabama, Mississippi and Louisiana outlawed further slave trade but allowed the system then in operation to continue; that is, while no further slave trade was encouraged, slave owning and all laws pertaining to slavery were to be maintained.

Slave holding was not confined to the South. Massachusetts at one time had 400 slaves; Rhode Island, the home state of ninety per cent of the American slave ships, held 333 Africans and 233 American Indians as slaves; Connecticut's Governor Leete reported "There are but a fewe servants amongst us and less slaves, not above thirty."

In 1644, with the Indian raids growing more and more ferocious upon the Dutch settlements at New Netherlands, Governor Stuyvesant considered arming African slaves and sending them to fight the Indians. New Jersey and Pennsylvania had but a scattering of

RUN away, on the 3d Day of *May* last, a young Negro Boy, named *Joe,* this Country born, formerly belonged to Capt. *Hugh Hist.* Whoever brings the said Boy the Subscriber at *Ediso,* or to the Work House in *Charles Town,* shall have 3 *l* reward. On the contrary whoever harbours the said Boy, may depend upon being severely prosecuted, by
Thomas Chisham.

TO BE SOLD *by* **William** Yeomans, (in *Charles Town* *Merchant,*) a parcel of good Plantation Slaves. Encouragement will be given by selling Rice in Payment, or any good Troopling saddles and *Furniture,* choice *Barbados* and *Boston* Rum, also Cordial Waters and Limejuice, as well as a parcel of extraordinary *Indian* trading Goods, and many of other sorts suitable for the Season. Time Credit, Security to be given if required There's likewise to be sold, very

Slave runaways were frequent. Notices were sent out and men hired to recapture them. They were hunted to the Canadian border where many fled after getting help from the Underground Railroad, a route which led escaping slaves from the South into the North and often into Canada itself.

St. Thomas, now a popular resort in the United States Virgin Islands, was once the greatest slave port in the western hemisphere. Upon the stone platform that now contains the colorful market place (top, left), slaves once stood for auction. Above is the bell which proclaimed the emancipation of all slaves on St. Thomas in 1848 under the new constitution of Danish king, Frederick VII. Slave revolts and rebellions were feared wherever there were slaves in the New World. Illustrated above is a scene from the battle of Palmares, Pernambuco, Brazil, which occurred in 1696.

slaves due to the influence of the Quakers who, with the aid of the abolitionists, were instrumental in wiping out slavery in New England. Most of the seaboard states became free states before 1800.

In the constant raiding and shipping, the destinations in the New World of most of the slaves has become obscured. The west coast of Africa—the Grain or Ivory and Gold Coasts—were most often plundered by slave traders. Some slaves, through the Portuguese and Arabs, came from the far east African coast. In any given area, there lived many and even hundreds of different tribes. Generally the slaves were called by the region from which they had come. The natives of Senegal, for example, were called merely Senegalese, but the Fulani, Mandingo and Kru tribes, to name but a few, lived in the same region.

It was seldom that the American colonies in the North took their slaves directly from Africa as the Southern colonies did. Most slaves found in the North had come first from the West Indies and were, in a sense, already used to bondage and did not always fight it. Those brought directly from Africa to the Southern mainland were responsible for the greatest and most ferocious rebellions.

It is believed that only one out of every twenty captured slave ever reached America. The available figures indicate that a higher percentage arrived here, but those figures, inaccurate from the start and illegal later, cannot be reliable.

Harriet Beecher Stowe (left), who brought the attention of the U. S. to slavery with Uncle Tom's Cabin, *has often been credited with starting the Civil War. The novel swelled the ranks of existing U. S. Abolitionists and thousands became involved in one way or another in having slavery abolished. Frederick Douglass (1817-1895) (above) was born into but escaped from slavery. An agent of the Massachusetts Antislavery Society, he helped recruit colored regiments to fight in the Civil War and was consulted by President Abraham Lincoln. This facsimile of a handwritten section of Lincoln's draft of the Emancipation Proclamation (below) was written prior to January, 1863.*

And by virtue of the power, and for the purpose aforesaid, I do order and declare that all persons held as slaves within said designated States, and parts of States, are, and henceforward shall be free; - - - - - -

And upon this act, sincerely believed to be an act of justice, warranted by the Constitution, upon military necessity, I invoke the considerate judgment of mankind, and the gracious favor of Almighty God.

(L.S.) Independence of the United States of America the eighty-seventh.

Abraham Lincoln

By the President;
William H. Seward,
Secretary of State

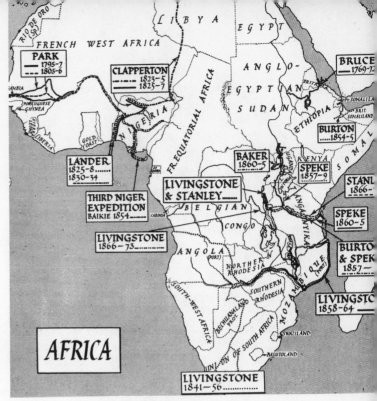

AFRICA

VENTURE INTO

THE HEART OF DARKNESS

James Bruce (1730-1794) (above) in addition to discovering the source of the Blue Nile traveled in Ethiopia (1768-1773). For over 100 years British explorers were attracted to Africa (map, right, shows routes). Two types of camels were available to Bruce and other explorers in the north of Africa (above): the Arabian with one hump (also called dromedary) and the Bactrian with two. Bruce found the Upper Nile (right) thick with fern and that it trickled down to a brook which was not the White Nile but the Blue. Enroute to the source, against a background of Kushite-Egyptian ruins, he may have seen an Ibis (right) which was worshipped and engraved as a sacred bird.

Ill-fated Mungo Park (left) went in search of the source of the Niger. Above village is typical of the ones he saw. During 1806 trip his boat was caught on the Busa Rapids.

To the Interior

The American Revolution from 1775 to 1783 and the Napoleonic Wars from 1796 to 1815 halted much of the exploration in Africa. By then, both Portugal and Spain had become second-class powers in the balance maintained in Europe. America had shown little if any interest in Africa.

Thus the British and French involved in the two wars, had little time and money with which to push back the African frontier. This is not to say that all ventures ceased; they did not. Maps were compiled in both France and England at this time, from information which drifted back or was written down by people who moved about the continent during the wars.

A big, hulking Scot, James Bruce, did as much as anyone to recreate interest in Africa. He landed in Cairo in July, 1768. His goal was to find the source of the Nile River. Egypt, at this time, was dominated by the Ottoman Empire. Napoleon's armies did not occupy it until 1798.

It took Bruce two years to find the headwaters of the Nile, but it turned out to be the source of the *Blue* Nile, not the famous Nile or *White* Nile. While his find was of great value, his work, *Travels to Discover the Source of the Nile* (five volumes), published in 1790, probably

stirred more interest in Africa than at any time since the century before.

So much interest was aroused in Africa that an organization, the African Association (later to become the Royal Geographic Society), was formed in London (1788) for the purpose of exploring the interior of the continent. The most famous of its leaders was a man named Mungo Park.

Park, a Scotch doctor, was 24 when asked by the African Association to find and explore the Niger River. There was some belief at the time that the Niger was the western branch of the Nile. He landed in Gambia in 1795, paused a few months to learn some Mandingo and to acquaint himself with African customs. After capture by and escape from Arabic tribesmen at Queira and surviving a sandstorm and a rainstorm, Park, living from one friendly African village to the next, came at last to the Niger on July 21, 1796. Making his way out of the jungle with some difficulty on foot and boat, Park lost his companion, Johnson, an African, and came back to England aboard an American slave ship, the *Charlestown*. The year was 1797 and Park was acclaimed a hero. He was the first known European to have seen the Niger.

Ten years later Park was back in Africa with a caravan that had forty mules in it. A Mandingo priest named Isaaco accompanied Park and his men as an interpreter. This second journey again brought Park to the Niger, but sickness and death had cut his force from forty to eight people. It is said that Park himself went mad and degenerated into a murderous man, killing Africans with such a ferocity that for fifty years after his death Africans told tales about him and retaliated by killing other white explorers. Park, a lieutenant Martyn and three other white men along with three slaves were lost when their boats caught on rocks at the Busa Rapids and they were attacked by Africans who slew them.

In 1823, seventeen years after Park's death, Captain Hugh Clapperton and Major Denham set out to finish the unlucky Scottish doctor's task: to trace the Niger to its source. They started their journey at Tripoli and crossed the Sahara going almost due south. Denham penetrated to the Shari River which runs into Lake Chad (Equatorial Africa) and Clapperton as far as Sokoto, about seventy-five miles from the Niger.

Two years later Clapperton tried again accompanied by twenty-three-year-old Richard Lander. Wounded in raids by unfriendly nomads and wracked with fever, Clapperton died at Sokoto.

With the entire Clapperton company dead, young Lander found himself at least three month's travel from the coast, and about the only known European in West Africa, save for occasional slavers. However, he did manage to get out and return to England where he edited Clapperton's papers and told his story and was rewarded with an expedition of his own.

He left England the second time in 1830, taking a brother, John. Canoeing on the Niger, they stopped at Busa and found what remained of Mungo Park's clothing. At a village further along the way, the Landers were captured and held for ransom. While held they learned from a Spanish slave captain that the brothers were only sixty miles from the Benue, one of the Niger tributaries. The young explorer succeeded in getting himself and his brother and the eight remaining survivors of the party out of the village and back to England on a Spanish slave ship where he became the first man to receive the medal of the Royal Geographic Society.

Napoleon, sailing secretly from Toulon, France, landed at Alexandria in 1798. He won the battle of the Pyramids but his fleet was destroyed by Nelson in the Battle of the Nile (above). Napoleon was preparing for a contemplated invasion of India but threats in Europe made him return in 1799. To the right: Capt. Clapperton and Maj. Denham.

Natives at left are typical of those who held Major Denham for ransom. Below, Richard and John Lander paddle down Niger.

The Nile and Beyond

The Nile River was a lodestone that drew the attention of many European explorers; the search for its source tempted the most daring adventurers. Among these was a remarkable man named Richard Burton (1821-1890); literate and fearless, he had led a thrilling life. One of his most incredible adventures was to penetrate remote Harar in Ethiopia (1854), disguised as an Arab; no white man had ever before made that trip.

Burton's non-conformist behavior startled staid Victorian England, but the British public eagerly bought his books describing his adventures in Africa. His chief companion on Burton's most perilous treks was a former fellow-officer of the East Indian Army, John Hanning Speke.

Speke had accompanied Burton to Harar in 1854 and later that year the pair explored Somaliland. There, in a clash with natives, both men were wounded by hostile tribesmen. Burton was lost for nearly four months, but finally rejoined Speke and the two men at last made their way out of the country.

In 1857 Speke and Burton again went to East Africa to further trace some of the waters they had found on their first trip and also to verify the many reports of lakes and streams beyond the Nile Valley, all of which had filtered back to England for a number of years.

Some probes were made near Mombasa, Kenya, but fever and difficulties with the authorities halted the expedition for a brief time. Pushing about 500 miles southward, they heard at Kaze from the natives that two lakes lay in or near the region: Nyasa and Ujiji (Tanganyika). These lakes in Tanganyika and Kenya were their discoveries.

Speke insisted that the Nile source was near Victoria, but Burton maintained it lay somewhere in Tanganyika. After some hot debate, the adventurers decided to split up; however, both became ill and were forced to go on together.

Near Ujiji, Burton's health became so poor from a violent ear infection that Speke went on to explore Tanganyika alone. He discovered Lake Victoria Nyanza on August 3, 1858. Upon coming back to pick up Burton, the two friends argued bitterly over the Tanganyika expedition, despite all the hardships they had mutually endured. At last it became obvious that they had to part company.

Speke abandoned Burton and left the country. Eventually Burton recovered, but his days of exploration were ended. He became well known in later years for his translation of the Arabian Nights and was also British consul in several African countries.

While America trembled on the brink of the Civil War, Speke, with a new companion, James A. Grant, returned to solve the riddle of the lakes and the source of the Nile. Speke's party of some 200 men left Zanzibar in October, frightening away in the process ten Africans who were fearful of being eaten by the Euro-

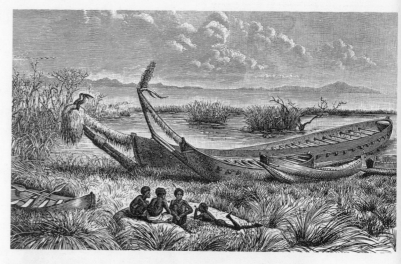

Opposite page: *East Africa was opened to the British with the explorations of Richard Francis Burton and John Channing Speke (top, left and right) in Somalia and Ethiopia in 1854. They returned again in '58, Burton discovering Lake Tanganyika and Speke, Lake Victoria. Burton continued in the British Consular Service for 20 years. From 1860-1863 Speke was again on the move—passing tribes migrating and gathering provisions from local people (center, left and right)—this time with Capt. James A. Grant (extreme left) and a sturdy group of 18 men (bottom). Traveling by boat (top, above), Speke met the Queen of Uganda (above) and Grant danced with the Ukulima (below).*

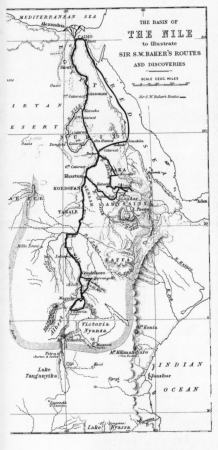

Traveling the same route as Speke and Grant, Sir Samuel and Lady Baker (left) saw villages being moved (above), lion hunts (below, left) and the Masai warrior (below). Note the Masai's customary, upright resting position.

Mercaldo Archives

So appalled was Baker at slave trade on the east coast that he headed an expedition from 1869-1873 to help stamp it out. A steamer (below) is hauled by natives through river grass as Baker approaches "The Stones" (below, right), a point at which the Nile flows out of Lake Nyanza.

peans. After a dangerous journey of nine months, Speke reached the banks of the Nile, moved on to the rapids where the river comes rushing out from the Victoria Nyanza and concluded with this and other reports that this indeed was the source of the Nile River.

During the course of this exploration, Speke and Grant disappeared into the unknown country and were lost for more than a year. In June, 1862, a sportsman and traveler, Sir Samuel Baker, in Africa with his beautiful young wife, was commissioned by the Royal Geographic Society to search for Grant and Speke.

The couple accepted the mission and did find the missing explorers. Grant and Speke told them of a great lake which they believed to be the source of the Nile. Baker and his bride pushed on to that body of water which they named Lake Albert Nyanza. Then, after crossing it on March 16, 1864, they endured incredible hardships to explore the region and finally reach Cairo late in 1865.

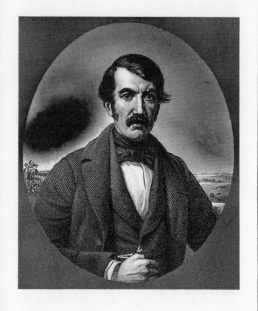

The Missionary

The man who unwittingly did more than anyone else to bring on the rush by European powers to grab colonies for themselves in Africa was a well-meaning Scotsman named David Livingstone. Born in 1813 in Blantyre near the Clyde River in Scotland, son of a devout man, a tea merchant, Livingstone worked fourteen hours a day in a cotton mill six days a week at ten years of age. He attended medical classes at the University of Glasgow, intent on becoming a medical missionary, a goal he achieved in 1840 after more study in London.

Livingstone wanted to go to China but the London Missionary Society sent him to Africa. He was a rugged man, possessed of a fundamental kindness and sometimes a flashing anger. In July of 1841 he entered Bechuanaland but the Dutch settlers, known as Boers, who populated that region refused to allow him to get on with his missionary work. He married Mary Moffat, a daughter of other missionaries in 1844. Livingstone continued his explorations, sometimes accompanied by his wife. In 1849 he discovered Lake Ngami and, two years later, the Zambezi River.

On what was perhaps his most exciting trip, Livingstone journeyed southward into Capetown to send his family back to England. Then with almost three dozen canoes and 160 men he set out to explore the Zambezi. While moving about the country, he always looked

When David Livingstone (top) completed religious and medical studies in 1840 he was sent to Bechuanaland in South Africa where Boers refused to let him work with Africans. Livingstone began his explorations (map), settling missions along the way, shortly after his marriage to Mary Moffat. By 1849 with 36 canoes (left) and 150 men, including two other Europeans—Oswell and Murray, he arrived at Lake Ngami in the northern Kalahari Desert (left, center).

35

Livingstone's trips were filled with danger. Once the missionary's boat was capsized by a hippopotamus robbed of her young (above, left) and another time his group was attacked by a lion (above) which crippled the explorer's arm. In 1851 Livingstone set out to explore the Zambezi River and its connecting water systems, finding the Tarn Bend (above); along the way he witnessed native elephant hunt (left). Considered Livingstone's greatest discovery was the falls (bottom, left) on the Zambezi, a tremendous sight he named for Queen Victoria in 1855.

for a site for a mission. He found the Kololo great friends and many of them accompanied him on his explorations. In September, 1852, after following the Bengo River to its mouth and back, he decided to continue on to the east.

With the help of the chief of the friendly Kololos, Sekeletu, he again made his way to the Zambezi, determined to explore all of it. From this point near Linyanti, Rhodesia, it took Livingstone two weeks to stumble upon what the Kololos and other tribesmen called "The smoke that sounds"—the incredible falls Livingstone named Victoria in honor of the Queen.

Livingstone said: "I . . . saw a stream of a thousand yards broad leap down a hundred feet and then become suddenly compressed into a space of fifteen or twenty yards. . . . The entire falls are simply a crack made in a hard basaltic rock from the right to the left bank of the Zambezi, and then prolonged from the left bank

Livingstone, one of the first Europeans to cross the continent, used the Ma-Robert (above), a steamer named for Mrs. Livingstone, upon the broad waters of the Zambezi. He found a variety of weapons and musical instruments used by the peoples in Central Africa. This group (above, right) shows horns, drums and xylophone-type instruments. To the right are three types of spearheads used in hunting.

away through thirty or forty miles of hills."

(Victoria Falls is about two-and-a-half times as high as Niagara, running from 256 to 360 feet high. Enough water goes over the falls every second to supply everyone in continental United States with three quarts. Its thunder can be heard ten miles away. The forests which surround the falls have been made into a government preserve for animals and birds.)

The missionary traced the Zambezi to its junction with the Loangwa then, half dead with fever, turned back to Quelimane on the east coast; he had been gone four years. Upon his return to England new maps were immediately drawn up; his reports of possible trade routes were absorbed and his notes on the flora and fauna of the region through which he'd traveled put to good use.

In 1857 his *Missionary Travels and Researches in South Africa* published, he left the London Missionary

During the 1858 expedition Livingstone was disturbed by the brisk slave trade which disrupted entire tribes along the Shiré and Zambezi rivers (above). The most cruel blow fell in 1862 when Mrs. Livingstone died at Shupanga on the Zambezi, only a little over 100 miles from the port of Quilimane. Natives cared for the grave (below).

The Chambezi River and its wildlife (above) was but one of the regions Livingstone explored upon his return to Africa in 1866. He had been appointed British Consul in Central Africa to wipe out slavery and to explore the Tanganyika water systems (right). On this his last trek into the heart of Africa Livingstone, crippled by fever, was carried to Ujiji (below) near Lake Tanganyika. At the lower, right-hand corner are Livingstone's relics.

Society and prepared to return to Africa under government auspices whose purpose was "to open up highways for commerce and Christianity to pass into the vast interior of Africa." He was also to serve as consul at Quelimane.

This trip out Livingstone was accompanied by his brother, Charles, an artist, a physician and a geologist. The vessel which transported them and the rest of the company to Africa was the *H.M.S. Pearl;* it dropped anchor near the mouth of the Zambezi on April 1, 1858.

For two years Livingstone and his party continued their explorations, completing the route of the Zambezi and discovering the Shire and Lake Nyasa. Mrs. Livingstone died of fever in 1862 and this, together with mechanical difficulties concerning their new ship, *The Pioneer,* threw Livingstone into severe depression.

Now there were frequent raiding parties of Africans around them. A harsh drought hit the region and Livingstone wrote in his journal: "Wherever we took a walk, human skeletons were seen in every direction." Most of the people in the party became ill and finally the expedition was recalled to England.

The Scotch missionary found his second welcome home somewhat less exuberant than the first. He did not linger long in England. In his travels in Africa he had seen that the slave trade was being carried on sometimes secretly, sometimes openly. He was in England only long enough to publish *Narrative of an Expedition to the Zambezi and Its Tributaries* in order to expose the Portuguese slavers (1865).

This time Livingstone started from Zanzibar, went inland toward the southern end of Lake Tanganyika and was stricken by fever. Undaunted, he had his bearers carry him in a litter to Lake Bangweulu. In 1866 he crossed Lake Tanganyika, seeking to reexamine the sources of the Nile. He disappeared into the bush and was not heard from again for years. No news came from Livingstone and the world presumed he was dead.

Relics of Dr. Livingstone.

a, Consular cap, worn by Dr. Livingstone to the date of his death. *b,* Consular sword worn by Dr. Livingstone. *c,* Leather pistol-case. *d,* Box containing forks and tea-spoons, used by Dr. Livingstone on his last journey, and brought home by his servants, Chumah and Susi.

Henry Morton Stanley

Soldier of Fortune

As late as 1871, James Gordon Bennett, Jr., the publisher of the *New York Herald*, still believed Livingstone to be alive. He felt it would be the journalistic sensation of the day if Livingstone were found under the auspices of the *Herald*.

Bennett enlisted the services of Henry Morton Stanley, a well known journalist, adventurer and explorer of Asia, Abyssinia and Crete, to undertake an expedition which would search for Livingstone.

Stanley, a Welshman, was thirty years old at the time. He had served in both the Confederate and Union armies during the American Civil War. As a Confederate he was captured at Shiloh in April, 1862, and gained his freedom by volunteering for the Union artillery. Discharged for medical reasons the same year, Stanley went on to become a journalist and traveler.

On March 21, 1871, the search for Livingstone got underway with much fanfare. At great expense Bennett had outfitted a fine expedition at a cost of some 4,000 pounds. Despite all the publicity, Stanley was determined to find Livingstone. He followed up a rumor that a white man had been seen encamped with a group of natives at the village of Ujiji near Lake Tanganyika on November 10, 1871.

After overcoming incredible hardships and hacking his way through impenetrable jungles, Stanley reached Livingstone's camp. The meeting between the two men produced a historic confrontation.

According to the accepted version, Stanley is supposed to have said, "Dr. Livingstone, I presume?" as he politely doffed his pith helmet.

Even as Stanley was meeting Livingstone, another expedition headed by W. Livingstone, youngest son of the missionary, Lt. L. S. Dawson and Lt. Henn (above) departed from London aboard the Abydos. *Having left the east coast of Africa in October, Stanley's expedition pressed inland bearing the American flag (right), since the search for Livingstone was under the auspices of the* New York Herald.

At any rate, while the actual conversation is not authenticated, Stanley found the lost Livingstone to successfully conclude one of the most remarkable rescue operations of all time.

Although Dr. Livingstone was terribly ill, by his own description a mere "ruckle of bones," Stanley could not persuade the missionary to quit Africa and return to England. Instead it was Stanley who remained—Livingstone was a persuasive man—and resumed explorations with the doctor when Livingstone recovered. Stanley and Livingstone jointly explored the north end of Tanganyika for two years then returned to the land of the Unyamwezi.

Stanley left, promising much-needed supplies for Livingstone and taking the missionary's journals and papers with him to England. Livingstone continued to wander, still in search of the source of the Nile. Illness struck him again, however, and he faded quickly. The last words entered in his journal were:

"Knocked up, quite, and remain—recover—sent to buy milch goats. We are on the banks of the Molilamo."

The date was April 27, 1873. Four days later he was found dead kneeling by his cot as though in prayer . . .

The expedition was then on the banks of the river Molilamo in Tanganyika. The bearers who had come to like Livingstone for his kindness and understanding removed his heart and buried it near the river. Then, wrapping his body in bark, they made the rugged journey to the east coast and there delivered it to Englishmen. They in turn conveyed the body to England where it still rests in Westminster Abbey.

In his search for Livingstone, Stanley grew interested in the vast potential of the wild country through which he was passing. After Livingstone's death, the *Herald* man spent two years exploring the Congo and became the first man to navigate the Congo River from the source to the sea. He also discovered Lake Edward and surveyed Lake Tanganyika (1874-1877).

Returning to Europe he tried to interest England in the possibilities of Africa. He had no success. As a result of this rebuff he returned to Leopold II, King of Belgium, who without hesitation grabbed the whole of what became the Belgian Congo—an area seventy-seven times the size of Belgium herself.

From 1879-1884 Stanley opened the Congo for Leopold. He built roads, set up trading stations and communications equipment. His unbounded energy was responsible for the founding of the Congo Free State which became a private estate for Leopold. The Belgian king administered these land with seldom equalled cruelty and unbridled tyranny. He was so severe that the Belgian people wrested the land from him and made it government property—the Independent State of the Congo (1908). But Belgium, little Belgium, had done so well in Africa that other European powers began to move in force back to the continent.

Opposite page: *The meeting on November 10, 1871, between Stanley and Livingstone (top) was highlighted by Stanley's "Dr. Livingstone, I presume?" Stanley tried to persuade Livingstone to return to England but the missionary refused and Stanley stayed. Together they explored northern Tanganyika (center, left), for Livingstone was pursuing the old theory that the Nile began there. Dr. Livingstone died April 27, 1873, on the Molilamo River. His brother, Charles, also a missionary died months later near Lagos, Nigeria. Livingstone had opened up Central and inland East Africa; he had discovered countless rivers and tribes. Without Livingstone, explorations in Africa might* have been delayed for a generation or two. This is the hut where he died (center, right). After leaving Livingstone, Henry Morton Stanley returned briefly to England and then headed his second expedition to Africa in 1872 (bottom, left). Five years later, after discovering Lake Albert Edward, circumnavigating Lake Victoria and Tanganyika and finding a falls in the Congo River which he named after himself, as well as the Stanley Pool (bottom, right), Stanley came to Boma (below, left) on the West African coast. The trek had not been without hazard; there had been many battles with strange tribes (below) with ivory traders and slave raiders (bottom of page).

In 1888 Stanley led a relief column to rescue German-born Eduard Schnitzer, known as Emin Pasha, the governor of Sudan, whose warrior subjects had risen in revolt. Later the indefatigable Stanley discovered the Ruwenzori Mountains known as the Mountains of the Moon which lay between Uganda and the Congo.

A short time later the explorer gave up this adventurous life and returned to England where he took up writing and turned to politics. He was successful at both ventures, publishing a number of widely read books on Africa. In 1895 Stanley won a seat in Parliament. He died in 1904 at the age of fifty-three, having experienced more adventure in his lifetime than almost any other man of his generation.

After the British, Stanley went to King Leopold II of Belgium (above) who was very interested in securing the Congo, not for Belgium but as a private estate for himself.

Commissioned by King Leopold to open up the Congo for its great wealth, Stanley used a steamer which had come overland in sections (above). With the vessel he was able to move swiftly across the vast Congo. In his travels he came upon the pygmies of the Ituri forest (left). Other explorers had found them but Stanley was intrigued by the way they used their poisoned arrows and spearheads (below) to kill game and strike fear into their enemies.

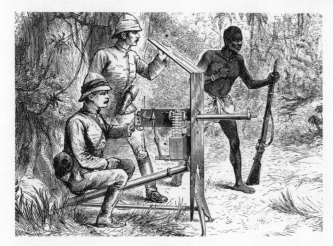

Stanley came out of seclusion in his English home in 1887 to lead his third expedition to search for the governor of the Sudan, Emin Pasha (above, left). The Pasha, cut off by the "Whirling Dervishes" or Mahadi fanatics, was believed to be in the lower Sudan at the edge of the Ituri forest. Pasha had studied medicine and ornithology and had traveled in Turkey before he went to the Sudan where he met "Chinese" Gordon. Pasha was credited before his death in 1892 with gathering the greatest amount of scientific data ever obtained in Africa. Stanley and Pasha reached safety in 1889. During his search for Emin Pasha, Stanley discovered the Ruwenzori mountains (above)— the "Mountains of the Moon"—which rose between the Congo and Uganda to 17,000 feet. In addition to the prefabricated steamer, Stanley brought other modern innovations to Africa. He is shown with the portable Maxim automatic machine gun (left), used successfully during the expedition to rescue Emin Pasha from Mahadi. Map (below) shows the routes of Stanley's three trips across Africa.

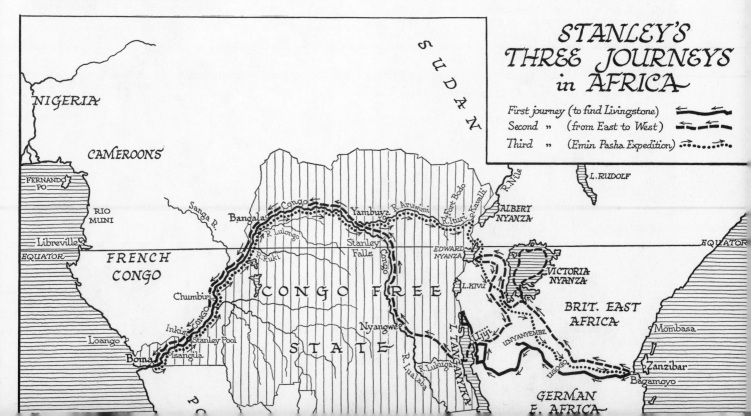

STANLEY'S
THREE JOURNEYS
in AFRICA

First journey (to find Livingstone)
Second " (from East to West)
Third " (Emin Pasha Expedition)

Later Pathfinders

Heinrich Barth (top, left) discovered the Binue or Benue River, a branch of the Niger, in West Africa in 1851. A view of the type of unprotected coastline which characterized West Africa near the equator is at right; Ghana is notable for its lack of natural harbor. Paul du Chaillu (above), a naturalized American from France who brought back the first gorillas (below, right) seen in America as a result of his explorations in West Africa from 1856-1859, was one of the first to explore Ashanti in northern Ghana and see the Fanti warriors (below) of that region.

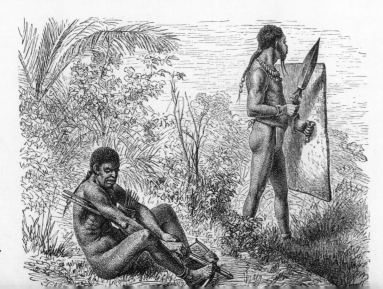

Mercaldo Archives

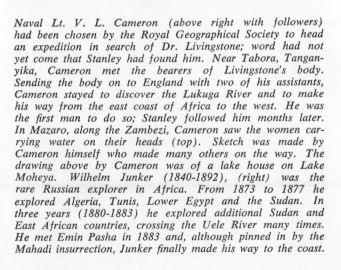

Naval Lt. V. L. Cameron (above right with followers) had been chosen by the Royal Geographical Society to head an expedition in search of Dr. Livingstone; word had not yet come that Stanley had found him. Near Tabora, Tanganyika, Cameron met the bearers of Livingstone's body. Sending the body on to England with two of his assistants, Cameron stayed to discover the Lukuga River and to make his way from the east coast of Africa to the west. He was the first man to do so; Stanley followed him months later. In Mazaro, along the Zambezi, Cameron saw the women carrying water on their heads (top). Sketch was made by Cameron himself who made many others on the way. The drawing above by Cameron was of a lake house on Lake Moheya. Wilhelm Junker (1840-1892), (right) was the rare Russian explorer in Africa. From 1873 to 1877 he explored Algeria, Tunis, Lower Egypt and the Sudan. In three years (1880-1883) he explored additional Sudan and East African countries, crossing the Uele River many times. He met Emin Pasha in 1883 and, although pinned in by the Mahadi insurrection, Junker finally made his way to the coast.

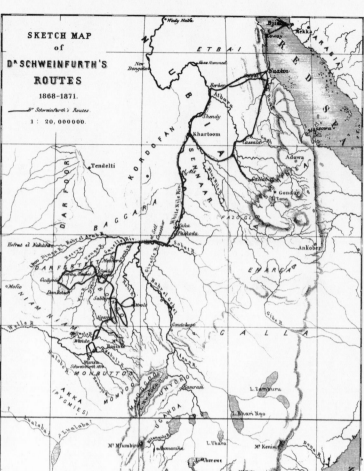

Above: *An explorer and botanist, Georg August Schwein-furth was born in Latvia in 1836. In addition to his brilliant botanical explorations of the Nile Valley (1864-1866) he discovered the Uele River—northeast quarter of the Congo Republic—in 1870. Four years later he founded a geograph-ical institute at Cairo and thereafter probed the desert between the Nile and the Red Sea for 12 years. He wrote* The Heart of Africa *(1874) and* Artes Africanae *(1875).*

Below: *Hermann von Wissman was born in Frankfurt, Ger-many, in 1853. In 1880 he went to Angola and from there crossed the continent to Zanzibar on the east coast two years later. Sent out by Leopold II of Belgium in 1884 he established stations in the Congo and the navigability of the Kasai River. He failed in 1892 in his effort to carry two dismantled steamers (below, left) overland to Lake Vic-toria. The author of many books on Africa, he died in 1905.*

Johann L. Krapf (above), a missionary and linguist, was born in Germany in 1810. He discovered Mts. Kilimanjaro (right) and Kenya in 1848 and 1849. Gustave Nachtigal (right) went to Africa for his health. Five years later, in 1868, he carried gifts from the Prussian king to the sultan of Bornu. He explored much of what is now independent Togo and Cameroon from 1870 to 1874. A year later he went to Egypt and then back to Germany. Made the German Consul in Tunis as well as the German Imperial Commissioner to West Africa, Nachtigal was responsible in 1884 for the German annexation of Togo and the Cameroon. He was born in 1834 and died off Cape Palmas in 1885.

OTHER IMPORTANT EXPLORERS

WILLIAM BALFOUR BAIKIE (1825-1864) a Scots surgeon and naturalist who on a Niger Expedition (1854) was shipwrecked. He made his way to Lokoja and there compiled a vocabulary of 50 Hausa (northern Nigeria, Mali) dialects. He also translated parts of the Bible into the Hausa languages. He died in Sierra Leone.

CHARLES T. BEKE (1800-1874), an English geographer, explored Ethiopia and Palestine. From 1847 to 1860 he published a series of works on the languages of Ethiopia and the sources of the Nile.

LOUIS GUSTAVE BINGER (1856-1936) explored West Africa, particularly the region north of the Ivory Coast. Established French protectorate and became governor of the Ivory Coast (1893). (French)

FRIEDRICH GERHARD ROHLFS (1831-1896) explored Morocco (1861-1862) crossed the Sahara from Tripoli to Lagos, Nigeria (1865-1866), Egypt (1865) and crossed the Libyan desert (1873-1874). (German)

THE ZULU:
BOLD WARRIORS

Even as Stanley, Livingstone and the parade of explorers snaked through Africa's jungles, traversed her rivers and scaled her lofty mountains; even as white soldiers guarded commercial routes and conquered one proud African tribe after another, African warriors girded to fight the white trespassers.

The most resolute warriors of South East Africa were the Zulu and of those bold tribesmen an almost legendary hero was a young Zulu king named Shaka. He was born in 1773 at a time when the Zulu were a sub-tribe dominated by the bellicose Umtetwas who were led by a bold and adventurous chief named Dingiswayo, known as The Wanderer.

Dingiswayo was more than an able warrior—he was something of a military genius and organized his young men into *impis* or regiments. No tribesmen in the jungle could stand against the Umtetwa *impis* and soon Dingiswayo ruled all Zululand.

Shaka, son of Usenzangacona, king of the Zulu, became Dingiswayo's protege. The youth lived, rode and fought with the mighty warrior chief and when Dingiswayo was slain in battle in 1818 the twenty-five-year-old Shaka became king of all the Zulu.

Using modern weapons stolen or bought surreptitiously from the British as well as improving ancient fighting methods and arms, the Zulu under Shaka swallowed up more than fifty neighboring tribes. He built a trained and disciplined army. Compulsory military service for all boys and men was instituted. A guard corps of 15,000 men able to move anywhere at a moment's notice was established.

In the various villages under his domain, Shaka had placed regiments of his best fighting men to man the forts. So strict was Shaka that if a regiment lost a battle he put the wives and children of the defeated soldiers to death. Whole families were slaughtered for a simple

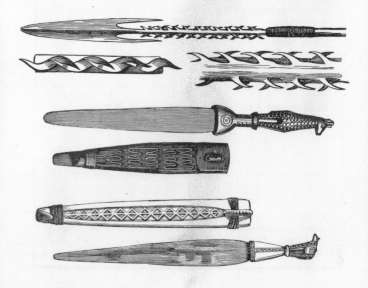

48

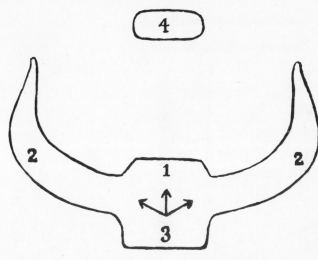

infraction. According to legend, he commemorated his mother's death by killing 7,000 people.

What Shaka was trying to bring out of all this cruelty was a Zulu nation strong enough to repulse the white settlers who were advancing and taking over the land; but it was difficult to communicate his hopes for the future to his people. Shaka was assassinated September 23, 1828. He was succeeded by Dingane, a close relative.

Under Shaka, the precision and daring of the Zulu and their sub-tribes had all but halted the advance of the Dutch settlers (Boers) who were moving in to the north. However, a sub-chief of the Matabele tribe, one Mzilikazi, developed a feud with Shaka and the embittered chieftain moved his people and cattle out of Shaka's jurisdiction, migrating farther north into the very country which the Boers had already penetrated.

Dingane who continued the great Zulu fighting tradition, adapted for his own use Shaka's method of fighting, a tactic called The Horn. In this formation the Zulu advanced upon or allowed the enemy to approach its crescent shape. In the center of the crescent was the main fighting force with some reserve in the distance. The "Horns" of the column then attacked the flanks of the enemy, engaged it, then loosed the main body for the kill. The formation was unstoppable for a number of years.

The Boers who had indeed pressed northward in 1835, the year of "the Great Trek" (very similar to American wagon trains of the Old West), had an easier

The Zulu horn attack formation (top): as soon as contact is made by the main body (1) troops begin to feed left and right into the flanks (2) in order to encircle the enemy (4). The Zulu reserves (3) are in a position to move up into the main body or out to the flanks. Zulu chief Shaka buried his mother's body (top, left) which was accompanied by live young women who would go with her on her journey and serve as handmaidens. Shaka unified Zulu people. Dingane was another powerful Zulu chief. Shown resting in his hut (below), he was a ferocious leader. He used Shaka's "horn" to successfully attack and massacre the Boers.

Opposite page: Young Kaffir chief (top) led his tribe in wars against the British in South Africa from 1877-1879. The assagai (left), weapons made of wood and metal, were at first long spears which were shortened for effective close-range use. The Hottentot (far left) erect a village.

49

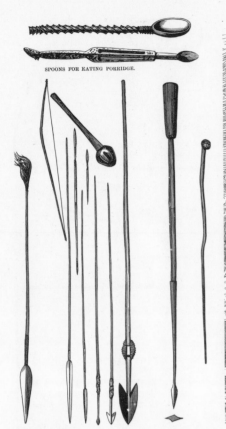

SPOONS FOR EATING PORRIDGE.

The Zulu were equally proud of their decorative spoons and assortment of clubs and assagai (above). The Matabele tribe in a war dance (above, right). Two warriors flee gunfire of British attackers (below) during Kaffir War. To the British "Kaffir" meant any native of South Africa.

time of it, for a while at least, with Dingane. He allowed them to enter Zululand (the area south of the Limpopo River) in 1837. The Boers were moving north to escape the influx of Englishmen. A year later he signed a pact guaranteeing the safety of the colonists in the Natal area (1838) but promptly set out to massacre them. He was defeated by Andries Pretorius, commandant-general of the Boer forces, December 16, 1838, and had to retire from the field.

A Zulu chieftain, Umpanda, betrayed Dingane and joined the enemy with 4,000 men in an effort to secure the Zulu crown for himself. Umpanda's treachery brought about the downfall of Dingane in 1840, whereupon he ascended the throne and concluded a semblance of peace with the whites.

The fighting then shifted to the north where Mzilikazi had emigrated. As the Boers pressed northward into land the Matabele considered their preserve, Mzilikazi launched fanatical war against them.

He had more than the Boers with whom to contend, however. Umpanda attacked the Matabele at the request of the white settlers. A fierce tribal war erupted and Mzilikazi pulled back across the Limpopo River, taking 5,000 warriors with him into what is now Southern Rhodesia. From his new stronghold, Makalanguland, the doughty Matabele chief raided Boer settlements and defeated them in pitched battles many times.

Back in the south, Cetewayo, who had succeeded Umpanda, was recognized by Great Britain as the king of the Zulu in 1872. Seven years later, angered by con-

50

Members of the British 90th Light Infantry disarm Africans (above, left) near the Kimberley diamond fields. Fingo tribesmen, who remained loyal to the British, fought against the Galeka and Gaika tribes. Zulu remained neutral. Mounted Fingoes escort Kaffir prisoners to town (above). At battle of Umzitanzi in the Transvaal, December 2, 1877, the British beat back the Galeka with small loss (below). Novelist Anthony Trollope held a light view of the Kaffir Wars; he felt there were few losses all around.

tinued British encroachments, he attacked and destroyed a British regiment of 12,000 men at Isandula.

Captured months later, he was imprisoned for three years, and sent to England in 1882. An unsuccessful attempt was made by the British to reinstate him on the throne; the Boers objected, preferring less war-like Zulu sub-chiefs for consideration.

Northward again, Lobengula (1833-1894), son of Mzilikazi, was friendly to the British for a time. When the British South Africa Company sought to extend its gold mining concessions granted by King Lobengula, however, the Matabele went to war. They attacked the Mashona, a sub-tribe still friendly with the whites. The British then joined the Mashona, slaughtering the Matabele with machine gun fire.

Lobengula retreated into central Southern Rhodesia, giving up his capital at Bulawayo. Except for a brief uprising quelled by Cecil Rhodes, South Africa saw the end of the Zulu Wars by 1896 and, like the American Indian, the Zulu were all but exterminated in the process of achieving peace on the frontier.

Great Britain was the indirect cause of the Zulu-Matabele wars. The "Great Trek" northward by the Boers in 1835 resulted from British power which had solidified by 1814 in South Africa. The Boers not only hated the British but also were disgusted at the rapport the British were trying to establish with the natives.

Though God-fearing people, they felt the British idea of raising the Kaffirs—the Africans of the region—to equality with whites was wrong and sinful.

THE
GREAT POWERS
GRAB
FOR AFRICA

Long before the Zulu and Kaffir Wars splintered the tribes in South Africa, European powers were chewing off parts of North Africa. France occupied Algiers (top) and Bizerte, Tunis (above) and by 1854 had acquired by conquest and exchange with England St. Louis, Senegal (below).

The French entered Algeria in 1830 to suppress Barbary pirates but after seventeen years the punitive expedition remained a full-scale occupation; Algeria became a French colony. Ten years later, Britain and France agreed on a division of West Africa. Britain wanted only a series of rich colonies. France on the other hand thought of a vast overseas empire.

France recognized the British claim to Gambia, and the British in turn, relinquished all claims to Senegal. As a result of military conquests in 1854, the French obtained in addition Dahomey and the Ivory Coast. The French also planned a casual occupation of the west central Sudan extending from Lake Chad westward. Great Britain, still unsure about the possession of colonies in Africa, once considered dropping all of them except Sierra Leone.

By now the full effects of the travels and maps made by Heinrich Barth (1821-1865) and other Germans had taken hold on Germany which, at first, had wanted no part of colonies in Africa.

While Great Britain was claiming that she had to extend inland from Sierra Leone, and France was concerned with holding her possessions, Germany in 1884 proclaimed the Protectorate of Togoland. This halted the eastward expansion of Great Britain and solidified the French colonies under French rule.

Meanwhile, Pierre Paul François Camille Savorgnan de Brazza (1852-1905), for whom Brazzaville in the Congo was named, had made a series of explorations to the Ogowe basin and discovered both the Alima and Likuala rivers. In 1879 the region he had explored was placed under French rule.

The Portuguese too were clamoring for a share of the Congo River outlet to the sea and at the International Congress of Berlin, 1884-1885, she was given Cabinda on the north shore of the Congo.

A year later Portugal, still pressing for claims in Africa, almost gained all the territory between Angola on the west coast and Portuguese East Africa thanks to France and Germany. Great Britain protested, however, and Portugal dropped her claims.

Many similar moves by European powers in Africa were counter-actions to halt other powers. No one cared about the tribal, language or custom lines of the African. For instance, at the time the Germans claimed Togoland they also claimed the Cameroons and Southwest Africa.

In 1859 a Frenchman, Vicomte Ferdinand Marie de Lesseps (1805-1894), organized a company for the purpose of building the Suez Canal; ten years later, after incredible hardships and tribulations, the "Big Ditch" was opened to world navigation.

The canal shortened the lines of commerce to the Far East and reawakened British interest in Africa. To help develop British mercantile holdings in the east, the British East Africa Company was formed in 1888 and, together with the Royal Niger Company and the British South Africa Company headed by Cecil Rhodes, secured British trade on the Dark Continent.

Senegal was the home of the maneless lion (above). Dahomey, the land of the Amazon (right), and the Ivory Coast were also French acquisitions. The Suez Canal, under construction from 1859-1869 (below), was opened by the heir to the British throne, Edward VII. View from Port Said at the Mediterranean end (above, right) shows ships rigged for both steam and sail in the days following the opening of the Canal which British purchased from Egypt in 1875.

Boers, Uitlanders

and Diamonds

With the seizure of the Cape Colony by the British in 1795, the Boers moved northward in 1835. A Boer family makes the "Great Trek" (top) in covered wagon and oxen into Zululand. Above is a Boer farm in the Orange Free State. The British thought the Boers "primitive and often a trifle dirty," and Boers believed the British soft, greedy. Although the Boers had been given some independence in the Transvaal with the discovery of diamonds in 1867, the British annexed the province in 1877. Kimberley, "The Big Hole" (below), was in Griqualand West at O.F.S. border.

The discovery of diamonds (1867) in the Kimberley district of the Cape Province in South Africa brought to a head the long series of conflicts between the British and the Boer "Voortrekkers" of Dutch descent. It was due to the British, in fact, that the Boers began their famed "Long Trek" to the north to escape political oppression in what they had considered their land.

After the succession of clashes with the British the Boers were finally granted a measure of independence in the region of the Transvaal (1852). Two years later, as a result of the Convention of Bloemfontein, the British withdrew from the lands north of the Orange River. The Boer settlers then organized the Orange Free State. In 1856 the organization of the South African Republic took place with Pretorius as president and Pretoria (founded 1855) set as the capital.

Then, with the disclosure of diamonds, the British returned, annexing the diamond region which had been under the rule of Chief Waterboer, a Zulu, but under the ultimate authority of the Orange Free State. While the Boers protested vigorously, it did little good. Some work had gone forward on the problems of a British-Afrikane federation, but the continued annexations of Britain nullified all the work. Finally the Boers in the Transvaal under Kruger, Joubert and Pretorius claimed a Boer republic and prepared to meet a British force sent out under Sir George Colley. The British were defeated and Colley killed. On April 5th, 1880, Britain concluded the Treaty of Pretoria, giving the South African Republic independence, but under the suzerainty of Britain. Paul Kruger, "Oom Paul" (1825-1904), became president of the Transvaal in 1883.

Kruger, a giant of a man whose family had been among the early Boer settlers, was one of the first

Afrikaners of prominence. He came up through civilian and military ranks to assume the presidency. A man of massive and legendary strength, he loved the land from which he worked so hard to wrest a republic.

There was another man, Cecil Rhodes (1853-1902), an Englishman, who came onstage at about this time. He was to influence the history of South Africa as much as Kruger and perhaps more since under Rhodes not only South Africa but parts of Rhodesia as well became industrial countries. Physically Rhodes was just the opposite of Kruger. A slim man who had been afflicted with tuberculosis, Rhodes came to South Africa for his health in 1870. The next year he moved to work a prosperous diamond claim with his brother in the Kimberley fields.

Rhodes who amalgamated the various diamond mines under the De Beers Mining Company (1888) seemed bent on bringing vast industry to the country.

Rhodes went to Matabele Chief Lobengula and had the chief sign over Matabeleland and Mashonaland. These are now the Rhodesias, named in honor of empire builder Rhodes.

This mineral empire extends from the Transvaal northward to the Congo and Tanganyika. The Zambezi River divides the north and south sections. Northern Rhodesia, larger than Texas, is twice as big as the southern section, but less populated. To move the wealth extracted from the gold and diamond mines Rhodes built railways from the fields to the cities. But the Boers in the Transvaal had but one rail outlet to the sea, the British having annexed Pondoland, Tongaland and then Bechuanaland in 1895. However Rhodes did not quite have all the gold in the Transvaal—but he wanted it.

Cecil Rhodes (above, left) was the man who made South Africa an industrial giant by combining gold and diamonds in his De Beers Mining Co. Political intrigues toppled him from power in 1896 and he returned to Rhodesia to start again. The diamond fields (above) were along the Vaal River. They differed from those in Australia and America, a British writer pointed out—the "dark-skinned race was available" for doing the hardest part of the digging. Fortune hunters came from all over the world. The rush flooded British markets; prices fell to 50% of value. The annexation of the Transvaal led to war (below) which did not end until 1881. Here Sir George Colley's troops climb Majuba Hill. Colley was killed in the Transvaal War

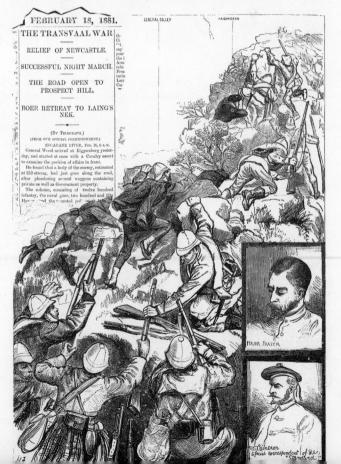

55

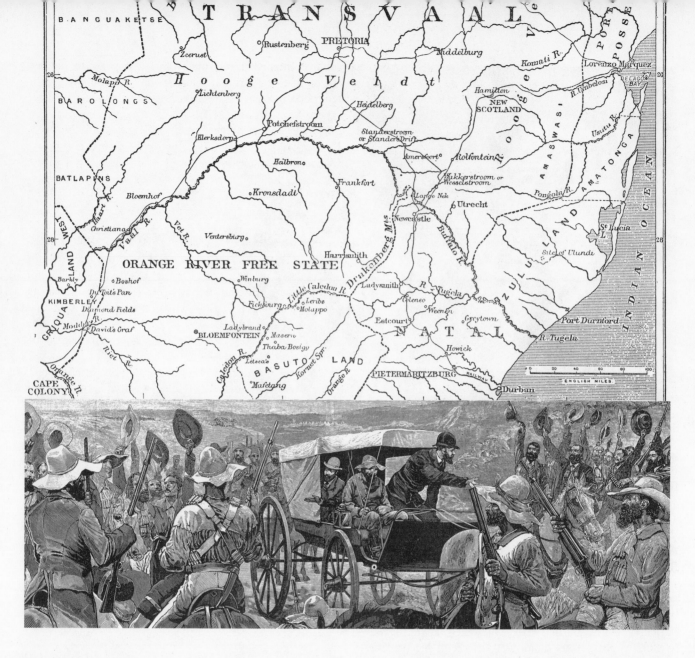

Map of Transvaal, Orange Free State and Griqualand West (top). President Brand of Transvaal brings message of peace (above). Discovery of gold in 1886 disturbed the uneasy peace. British held Transvaal under suzerainty. The De Kaap Fields (below) was one of the largest gold reefs.

In 1896 after trying to goad the Boers into a fight, Rhodes with help and smuggled arms engineered a coup, later called the Jameson Raid. The purpose was to revolt against Kruger and the Boers and hopefully with some approval from Britain turn the Transvaal back into British hands. Some of the people involved in the raid were called Reformers—they wished a change in government and were mostly British and lived in the Transvaal. Dr. Leander Starr Jameson was one of Rhodes assistants. After weeks of cloak-and-dagger activity, the Reformer forces marched on Johannesburg only to find the Boers ready. Jameson was captured and Rhodes, for his part, was forced to resign as prime minister of Cape Colony, January 6, 1896. He then devoted his efforts to developing the Rhodesias. He later died of heart disease and was buried in the land upon which he had worked for so long, leaving millions upon millions of dollars which was the basis for the famed Rhodes Scholarships. U. S. Supreme Court Justice Byron White was a Rhodes scholar.

The Boer War

The Boer War was inevitable. All ports to the sea were held by British colonies which completely surrounded the Boer states, except for a stretch of Portuguese Mozambique.

Under some prodding by Cecil Rhodes, his De Beers Mining Company and England, the Boers had given some thought toward friendship and federation with the British; all of this went up in smoke when the Jameson Raid occurred upon the Transvaal.

In the Boer Cape colony there was great mistrust of the British. The Orange Free State sided with Kruger and the other Boer colonies united for war.

The Britons living in predominantly Boer regions (they were called Uitlanders or Outlanders) did not keep out of the action. In April, 1899, a petition bearing the signatures of 20,000 Uitlanders, complaining that they were being mistreated and that Great Britain was suffering a loss of prestige at the hands of the Boers, was delivered to London.

Sir Alfred Milner, South African High Commissioner, was convinced that the Boers intended expelling the British, and "Oom Paul" Kruger was similarly certain the British meant to drive out the Boers. On October 12, 1899, the Boers moved against the British. While the latter were weak in number to begin with, eventually some 500,000 troops from all over the Empire landed in South Africa. The Boers, on the other hand, had only 35,000 men when the war started and once

By order of President Paul Kruger (top, left) 35,000 Boer troops began the Boer War October 12, 1899. Here (above left) we see a slashing saber charge by British cavalry. Used to fighting from most rugged terrain, Boers successfully used this method against British (left). Under Gen. Lekuku, the Bamangwate of north Bechuanaland (bottom, left) fought with the British during war. The Essex Regiment hauls its cannon to the crest of Coles Kop (below).

Translation.

£25
(Twenty-five Pounds stg.) REWARD is offered by the
Sub-Commission of the fifth division, on behalf of the Special Constable
of the said division, to anyone who brings the escaped prisoner of war
CHURCHILL,
dead or alive to this office.

For the Sub-Commission of the fifth division,
(Signed) LODK de HAAS, Sec.

Mafeking, under siege by Boers from start of the war (above), was relieved after nine months without aid. Named "Long Cecil" (insert, above) after Rhodes who was trapped in the De Beers Works at Kimberley, gun blazed back at Boers. Facsimile at right shows reward offered for Sir Winston Churchill. 9th and 12th Lancers sweep to the relief of Kimberley early in 1900 (below). Gen. Piet Cronje who had decimated British troops in both Transvaal and Boer Wars surrendered February 27, 1900 (bottom), when his 4,000 men were trapped. Fighting went on until 1902.

the British reinforcements were flowing into the country the Boers were badly outnumbered. When the Boers made their first moves they besieged Ladysmith, Mafeking and Kimberley, trapping Cecil Rhodes in the latter.

British reinforcements under Sir Redvers Buller, commander of the British Forces, arrived and advanced only to be thrown back by superior Boer marksmanship and by their German-made artillery. The Boers had excellent cavalry which inflicted many casualties on the slow-moving British. British losses shocked the Empire, though in today's warfare they would be considered slight.

Lord Roberts of Kandahar, known as "Bobs" to his men, was made the new commander. Lord Kitchener of Khartoum fame became his chief of staff. Together they made their objectives Bloemfontein, then Pretoria. Piet Cronje, the Boer commander, was trapped in a shift of his troops and had to surrender 4,000 men. Meanwhile, Kimberley had been relieved by General French and on February 16, 1900, Buller himself relieved Ladysmith. Roberts, continuing his onslaught across the countryside, took Bloemfontein in March and Johannesburg at the end of May. Pretoria fell early in June. An eight-month-long Boer siege of Mafeking was lifted under these blows. The Orange Free State collapsed and was promptly annexed by the British who believed the war to be over.

No sooner had Buller and Roberts left Africa than hostilities flamed anew, this time as a guerrilla action. The Boers formed striking units known as "Commandos" and lashed out against Natal but were subdued by General French. Other commandos using snipers and wearing plain clothes which blended into the landscape harassed the British until March 23, 1902, when the Boers asked for peace.

Friction Before World Conflict

Meanwhile, the Germans in 1892 moved into Southwest Africa. Under the Germans the Herero population decreased from 85,000 to 15,000; the cattle dwindled from 50,000 to absolutely zero. In the east along the Kenya plateau the Germans also had been building railroads. The work came to a halt with the outbreak of World War I.

Prior to the war, Britain had been active in the north of Africa as well as in the south; the French too had well defined plans for large additional pieces of the continent. In 1883 France took over a section of Somaliland, which held an important position near Bab el Mandeb near the southern tip of the Red Sea. The French planned to extend themselves eastward and northward from their colonies in Senegal and Niger. Then they would strike straight down from the Barbary Coast and allow these lands in the west to meet.

For their part, the British were eyeing Egypt which was a self-sustaining section of the Ottoman Empire. When Mehemet Ali, the Turkish Viceroy of Egypt, died in 1849 the ensuing anarchy gave Britain in 1880 the opportunity to intervene in Egypt, her dependencies, the Sudan and that portion of Somaliland which rested on the sea. The campaign of Horatio Herbert Kitchener (1850-1916) in the Khartoum region (1898) cleared out the Ottomans, made Egypt self-sustaining again—but under British protection. Kitchener was made governor of the Sudan and, so the Sudanese would never forget the might of the British, he had Khartoum laid out in the pattern of the union jack, the British flag. Kitchener was lost at sea, strangely enough, during World War I.

The success of the Kitchener campaign immediately put a stop to all French plans for moving westward from Somaliland. With headquarters for French influence in Africa in Algeria, the French in 1881 extended protection to Tunisia to end the possibility of Italian colonization there.

As the world geared itself for World War I, many regions in Africa had become more or less settled and divided among the European nations.

Spanish Morocco had come about through original claims and some concessions by the Spanish to the French. Italy, arriving late in Africa, had to content herself with sparse northern sections of the continent. When she plunged into Ethiopia in 1896, to place it under her protection, she was soundly thrashed at the battle of Aduwa which pitted Italian military technology against half-armed Abyssinians. It would take until 1936 for the Italians to avenge this defeat. The Red Sea bases Italy had acquired in 1880 stood near Bab el Mandeb and from these Italy extended the mantle of her protection over Eritrea and Somaliland.

As British and Boers fought, Italy sought land in Ethiopia only to be beaten at Adua in 1896 (above). The British drove out the Ottomans and remained in Egypt. Here (above, right) Lancers ride through battle maneuvers. Charles "Chinese" Gordon Pasha (right) stamped out slave trade in Sudan as governor. He died battling Mahadi worshippers in 1885. In 1892 Sir Herbert Kitchener (far right) began to roll back the Mahadi and in 1898 captured city of Khartoum.

To halt colonization of Tunisia by Italians, the French extended protection in 1881. French troops stand guard above. The British launched a two-pronged expedition north to Kumasi late in 1895 (see map) in order to bring the Ashanti warriors of the Gold Coast (Ghana) under the Crown. A British column of soldiers and carriers penetrate interior Nigeria on the Benin expedition of 1897 (below). The Beni sacrificed hundreds to stave off invasion. First large quantities of Benin art captured. At the turn of the century Germans in East Africa (left, below) were trying to use zebras as mounts instead of horses which died.

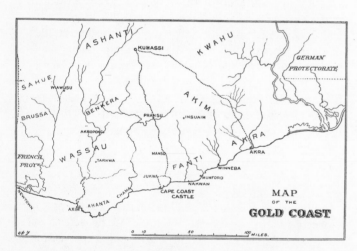

MAP
OF THE
GOLD COAST

0 10   50   100 MILES.

AFRICA
GOES TO WAR

A French Ghoum from North Africa (pictured above) fights in a European street with the Allies during World War I.

During the summer of 1914, Europe's great powers —England, France, Germany, Austria and Russia— clashed in the grimmest struggle of the twentieth century —the First World War. Europe was shaken by an earthquake of artillery and gunfire; but even as war erupted in distant Europe, its effects were felt throughout Africa.

In August 1914, only two weeks after the war had begun in Europe, a joint Franco-British force smashed the Germans in Togoland, securing that rich region by August 26, 1914. From South Africa, General Louis Botha aided by General Jan Smuts led a British army into German Southwest Africa after crushing a brief rebellion by Boer dissidents who hoped to overthrow British rule. Hardly a dozen years earlier Generals Botha and Smuts had fought vigorously against the British.

General Botha's invasion of German Southwest Africa started on January 5, 1915, and continued in an unbroken series of successes, through jungle and swamp, rains and floods. By July, 1915, all German opposition was broken and the vast territory was in British hands. There was severe fighting in the Cameroons and the German Congo as well. The hardest struggle, however, took place in German East Africa where, under Paul von Lettow-Vorbeck, barely 5,000 men of whom only five per cent were Europeans continually repelled, engaged and then evaded more than 130,000 British troops. The Germans put up stubborn resistance from September, 1914, until June, 1915.

Southwest Africa, held by Germans, was attacked by an expeditionary force from South Africa led by

Generals Christiaan De Wet and Maritz—other Old Boers. Then with Botha operating in the north, down from the Cameroon, and Smuts knifing up from the south, the British brought the fighting in Southwest Africa to an end at the battle of Gibeon and upon the acceptance of the capital, Windhoek. The defeats suffered by Germany in World War I ended that nation's state in Africa.

Most of the troops on both sides were native Africans. In all, more than 200,000 Africans saw action during World War I not only on their native soil but also on the Western Front where Senegalese, Moroccans, Ghoums and other Africans fought courageously and honorably with the European colonial powers.

The League of Nations which was created by the Treaty of Versailles in 1919 took up the claims of the Allied Powers for the division of the German colonies in Africa and also the consideration that a new kind of colonial government would be instituted throughout all of Africa. All affected member states agreed to League surveillance and that the administration of a colonial power would end when the community being governed showed it had the capacity for self-government. Belgium, the Union of South Africa, France and

In East Africa, fighting raged near Mt. Kilimanjaro (above). At left is Jan Christian Smuts, soldier and statesman. Below, pro-British forces under former Boer generals De Wet and Maritz take victory parade formation in South-West Africa.

Great Britain received African mandates from the League; all were former colonies of Germany, of course. Italy received nothing.

The division was as follows:

Great Britain—Tanganyika, Togoland
Belgium—Rwanda-Urundi
Union of South Africa—South-West Africa
France—Cameroon, Togoland

The mandatory powers agreed to adhere to tribal lines and lands; to aid wherever possible to the achievement of self-government. There were obvious breaches in these agreements but there was some progress. The French and British permitted and encouraged education of select groups within and without Africa.

Quite suddenly the modern world began to take notice of Africa.

The sculpture of Africa, for example, attracted the art capitals of Europe. Archeological expeditions continued in the Nile Valley and along the fringe of North Africa; the search for the earliest man went on, mostly in East Africa.

A former American President, Theodore Roosevelt, went on a year's big game hunt in East Africa in 1909 and five years later published his studies, *Life Histories of African Game Animals.*

This was also the year (1914) Edgar Rice Burroughs published *Tarzan of the Apes,* the first in a series of twenty-three books about the heroic Tarzan in the jungles of Africa. These works were so popular that they were translated into fifty-six languages and contributed immensely to the misconception of Africa and her peoples. The last in the series, *Tarzan the Magnificent,* was published in 1939.

Africa Between the Wars

Porters (above) outward bound on safari. Former President Theodore Roosevelt and son Kermit atop buffalo kill (left). Edgar Rice Burroughs (below, left), the creator of Tarzan. Mrs. Osa Johnson (below) astride one of her rhino kills.

These Riff tribesmen (above) under Abd-el-Krim resisted the Spanish in Morocco for over a dozen years. Crated African animals (above, right) prepare to leave Mombasa, Kenya. Dr. Albert Schweitzer (below), clergyman, philosopher, physician and musician, has been director of Lamaréné hospital in Gabon since 1913. Nobel prize winner, 1952.

Martin and Osa Johnson thrilled Americans in the 1930's with films of their trips. They photographed the vanishing wildlife of Africa for the American Museum of Natural History. They began the task in 1924 and completed it in 1929.

East Africa attracted American novelist Ernest Hemingway who, in 1935, described the excitement of big game hunting in *The Green Hills of Africa*. Some of his short stories had similar settings.

Frank "Bring 'em Back Alive" Buck became a sensation in the '30s for his daring captures of African animals for zoos around the world.

Pitchblende, discovered in the Belgian Congo in 1915, was mined until the late 1930's. When Sir Edward Sengier, owner of the Union Miniere du Haut Katanga, learned that the United States needed uranium to beat the Germans to the manufacture of atomic weapons, he reopened the mine and shipped more than 1,000 tons of uranium ore to a New York warehouse where, when war came, it was ready for use.

Italy invaded Ethiopa and became more firmly entrenched along the northern coast of Africa. In the mountains of Morocco, the Spanish army carried on an embarrassing war with the Riffians which lasted for twelve years, ending finally with the help of the French army in 1927. Some of these same Moroccan troops were used by the Nationalist government of Spain to wage the Civil War of 1936-38. The Moroccans were called "The Army of Africa" and the Civil War in its early stages could not have been won by the Nationalists without them.

Between the great wars some of the Africans who became leaders of their countries in the 1950's, studied in England and America. Among them were President Nkrumah of Ghana, Prime Minister Azikiwe of the eastern region of Nigeria, and Dr. Hastings Banda, nationalist leader of Nyasaland.

With the German armies maneuvering in Europe, the stage became set for World War II. It would affect Africa as well.

Africa Fights Again

Late in November, 1942, the Army of the United States launched *Operation Torch* along the beaches of North Africa at Casablanca, Algiers and Oran. Infantrymen and Rangers swarmed ashore in what was the first American invasion of Africa since 1803, when the fledgling United States had fought the Barbary pirates and American marines had marched across the desert to the stronghold of the enemy.

Operation Torch was designed to wrest the top of Africa from the Axis Powers, Germany and Italy. It marked the first large-scale entry of U. S. ground forces in the tense European-Mediterranean Theatre and was the initial test of Commander-in-Chief of Allied Forces Dwight D. Eisenhower. The North African campaign, whose battle lines stretched from Casablanca 1,200 miles eastward to Tunisia, also introduced such fighting generals as George Patton and Omar Bradley.

World War II had come to Africa long before *Operation Torch,* however. In August, 1940, shortly after the fall of France, Italian troops seized both British and French Somaliland and a huge Italian army marched from Libya across the Egyptian border to menace the Anglo-Egyptian Sudan.

For a time it seemed that an Italian victory was imminent; but the British soon struck back violently. In Egypt, British forces under General Sir Archibald Wavell smashed the Italians led by Marshall Rodolfo Graziani. As the Fascists reeled other British and native troops drove the enemy from East Africa. By May, 1941, Italy had lost all her African colonies including Ethiopia, which Mussolini had conquered in 1936.

When France fell in 1940 the Free French Forces, organized by General Charles de Gaulle, continued the fight from Brazzaville at the mouth of the Congo River.

The North African campaign was far from ended. German troops—the vaunted Afrika Korps—were

Not since 1803 when Capt. Bainbridge aboard the frigate Philadelphia (above) battled the Barbary pirates of Tripoli with Lt. Decatur (above) did Americans fight in Africa. Decatur returned to Tripoli in 1815 as commodore, released U. S. prisoners. AP photo of Gen. Erwin Rommel (at left, below) observing from atop tank in North Africa in 1942.

N. Y. Public Library, Picture Collection

U. S. forces land near Algiers to begin roll-back of Germans (above). U. S. battleship Rodney with destroyer escort, protects landing at Oran, Algeria, in one phase of Operation Torch *(below).* Opposite page: *Top, C-47 hustles supplies across Egypt's pyramids to aid Allies. Center, left to right, General of Army Dwight Eisenhower with British Field-marshal Montgomery, "Old Blood and Guts" Gen. George Patton, Jr. and Gen. Omar Bradley also stood out in* Torch. *Bottom, F. D. R. and "Winnie" issue a communique with high-ranking officers in Casablanca after Allied victory in Africa.*

rushed to aid the Italians. The Afrika Korps and its leader, Field Marshal Erwin Rommel, waged see-saw warfare against the British. Rommel earned for himself the nickname "Desert Fox." However, the Fox had his tail clipped by a dour Scotsman, Field Marshal Sir Bernard Montgomery.

Rommel had advanced within striking distance of Alexandria by the autumn of 1942. His farthest penetration was to El Alamein only sixty miles west of Alexandria; there the Axis advance was stopped. On October 23, 1942, Montgomery unleashed the British Eighth Army, the so-called "Desert Rats," in a powerful counter-attack which proved to be the turning point of the war's African phase.

Rommel was soon caught between the Americans and Monty's advancing troops. He was ordered by Hitler to stand fast although military logic demanded that his position be abandoned. When the war ended in May, 1943, with the Allied victory, the stage was set for future struggles which in a sense would be even more demanding than the slashing, bruising warfare between the Allies and the Axis.

The African people had felt the spark of freedom. More than 500,000 of them had served in the Allied forces in Africa, Europe and the Pacific. And now all the peoples of Africa were reaching for freedom and independence. For them, no sacrifice would be too great when liberty was the goal.

UHURU!

President Gamal Abdel Nasser of Egypt (above). Ex-Chief Albert John Luthuli (below), President General, African National Congress, South Africa. Nobel prize winner, 1961.

At the end of World War II only four African countries were independent: Liberia (1847), The Union of South Africa (1910), Egypt (1922) and Ethiopia (a monarchy extending back to Biblical times). Seventeen years later thirty-two nations would achieve independence.

The withdrawal from the often hard ties of colonialism was not always easy. Frequent changes in government took place, in Egypt for example, which culminated in Gamal Abdel Nasser's rise to power in 1952. Four years later when he nationalized the Suez Canal, British and French troops poured into the area and a major war was only narrowly averted.

The crushing policy of Apartheid came to South Africa when the Nationalist Party, composed of Boers, began to rule in 1948. It was this group which pressed hard for the separation of the Bantu peoples from the whites. This policy has angered most of the independent countries of Africa and could at any time flame into a war between South Africa and the nations of the north. While the African National Congress has been outlawed, it still functions underground, although constant, repressive new laws are drawn up against it. It is out of this atmosphere that Chief Albert Luthuli, head of the ANC and a Zulu, came to win the Nobel Peace Prize in 1961—the first African, black or white, to do so.

Kenya which has seen the steady rise of Nationalist leader Tom Mboya was rent with the raids of the Mau-Mau terrorists in 1952. Jomo Kenyatta, said to have been the Mau-Mau leader, was jailed by the British and released in 1962 an old and tired man. Mboya, who has often visited America, stressed "One Man, One Vote" in his campaigns, thus hoping to offset the power which has always been held by the whites. A noted American attorney, Thurgood Marshall, was invited to Kenya in the late 1950's to draw up the constitution of Mboya's party, preparatory to approaching independence. Zanzibar, adjacent to Kenya, was also moving toward freedom.

Algeria, independent only since 1962 after the eight-year war with France, faces internal trouble. One faction headed by Ben Kedda, urges that Algeria continue commerce with France. The leader of the opposition group, Ben Bella, wants nothing more to do with France.

The Ghana government of Dr. Kwame Nkrumah has come under severe criticism since it came to power on March 6, 1957, for one-party control. Some members of a barely formed opposition have been jailed or exiled from the country. However, it has been argued that Nkrumah's strong handedness was necessary to guide the country through the birth pangs of independence.

The federation of the Rhodesias and Nyasaland, the largest non-independent areas, have problems similar to those of Kenya. Manowa Chirwa, a leader of some questionable talent, gave way to Dr. Hastings Banda

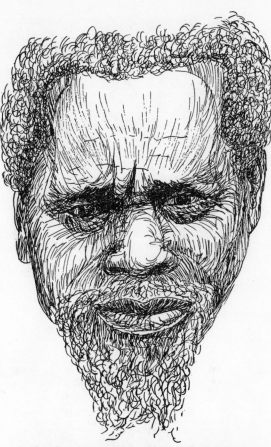

Kenya Nationalist leader Tom Mboya (above) and former Vice-President Richard Nixon confer in Washington. Jomo Kenyatta of Kenya (right) was alleged leader of 1952 Mau-Mau terrorists and predecessor of Tom Mboya. Dr. Kwame Nkrumah (below), President of Ghana, at the U. N. Julius K. Nyerere, Nationalist leader of Tanganyika (below, right).

American Committee on Africa — Sketch by R. H. Sargent

United Nations

United Nations

whose rallying cry, "Kwaca!" (the dawn), has built up in Nyasa tremendous momentum for independence. Like many African leaders, Dr. Banda was jailed for his political activity and then released on the demands of his people. White opposition to an independence which would give the black Africans equal opportunity is nearly as strong as it is in South Africa.

So poorly prepared were the people of the Belgian Congo when independence came that it will take some years before the tumult and misunderstandings cease. One of the wealthiest countries in Africa, the Congo may always be a trouble spot, unlike Nigeria which has a great deal of wealth of its own and has been blessed with eminent leaders and administrators.

When Tanganyika became independent in December, 1961, cautious, soft-spoken Julius K. Nyerere stepped down as the Nationalist leader to allow Rashidi Kawawa to become prime minister. Nyerere devoted himself to TANU (Tanganyika African National Union). Tanganyika's transition from a colony to an independent country has been smooth.

If there is one perpetually boiling volcano in Africa, it is the rule of the Portuguese over their two large colonies, Mozambique and Angola. Members of the Algerian Army of Liberation, even while they were engaged in war with France, were serving as guerrilla instructors to Angolan resistance fighters.

Those close to the scene of action predict that rebellions and even open war between the Angolans and the Portuguese is near. Holden Roberto is the president of the Union Populations of Angola (UPA) and the leading Nationalist.

Uganda, which lies west of Kenya, secured its independence in October, 1962. While there is some opposition to the plan, she probably faces some sort of federation with Kenya when the latter's independence comes.

Only nine per cent of the total population lives in those countries which have not yet moved toward independence. They live in an area which comprises but eighteen per cent of the continent. Nevertheless the cries of "Uhuru!" (freedom) and "Kwaca!" (the dawn) continue.

Critics of the massive move toward freedom say that by and large the African is not prepared for it. The African answers that first he must have freedom and then he will wrestle with the problems any new nation must face. In the seventeen years since the end of World War II, the face of Africa has changed quickly, dynamically. And the changes are still being made.

Photo not released until now shows Union Populations of Angola combat team with Algerian instructors (top). Holden Roberto (center), President of Union Populations of Angola, which is opposed to Portuguese rule. Dag Hammarskjold (left), United Nations Secretary-General until his death in 1961 Congo plane crash. (U. Thant is seen in background.)

STRIDES TOWARD INDEPENDENCE

Leading statesmen from all over the world attend the U. N. General Assembly (above). Left to right are: Gamal Abdel Nasser, Dr. Sukarno, Jawaharlal Nehru, Dr. Kwame Nkrumah and Mr. Saeb Salaam. The body of the late U. N. Secretary-General, Dag Hammarskjold (bottom of page), is carried to a waiting plane at Salisbury airport for its journey to Sweden.

Technology, which Africa sorely needs, and national gain go hand in hand with politics. How will the new nations realize their potential? Will Africa become a continent of little nations differing in custom and laws and conduct like the Balkan states of Europe before World War I?

These are questions which the impatient west asks.

The west forgets that Africa and her newly independent states are new only to this particular time. Her leaders are men bred of both Africa and the west, and their perspectives are vast. One need only remember that when William the Conqueror invaded Britain in 1066, Egyptian, Ethiopian and some central African peoples had a history of several thousand years. The roots of the great inland empires of Bornu, Songhai, Mali and Ghana were coming to vine at the time Christ was born; the incredibly mysterious East African civilizations had already flourished and waned, leaving few clues behind.

More than a hundred years before King John was brought to bay at Runnymede to sign the Magna Charta, al-Bakri (1040-1094) observed in an African kingdom that the king himself "gave audience to his people to listen to their complaints and set them to rights." In our modern day the inability of European powers to wean themselves from Saharan oil or Angolan coffee and North African naval bases presents a stumbling block to those nations desiring complete independence. Adverse racial attitudes also present the threat of violence which could seriously involve the entire continent.

There can be little doubt, however, that Africa is in the modern world. The European Common Market has already admitted sixteen of the new African states. Through international health organizations the nations of Africa are quelling illnesses which for centuries have taken a heavy toll of life. Crash programs are continuing to get qualified educators and technicians to Africa. The Peace Corp personnel augments these professionals. Finally, African nations have moved forward into the space age. Not only did Nigeria provide a tracking site for the orbital flight of Col. John Glenn but Ghana was in June, 1962, the host for an international conference on the effects of nuclear fallout.

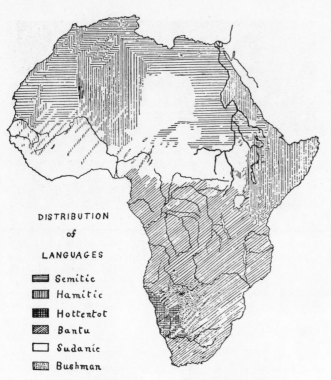

DISTRIBUTION
of
LANGUAGES

▤ Semitic
▥ Hamitic
▦ Hottentot
▨ Bantu
▢ Sudanic
▦ Bushman

PEOPLES,
PLACES
AND CUSTOMS

Map shows rough distribution of languages in Africa. Bushmen faces (above) are a child and an adult. Children are watched and raised by entire group, not only by parents. Bushwomen pause at a Kalahari water hole (below) to fill ostrich eggs.

BUSHMEN

These small groups form Nomadic bands in the Kalahari Desert. They build no living quarters, but reside in caves or in the open with any natural shelter available.

There is no agriculture in this society and the Bushmen have no cattle, although at one time they robbed cattle from the Boers as they crossed Bushmen territory.

The Boers were partly responsible for driving these small yellow people into the desert. Water is the most important single commodity. Bushmen store it in ostrich eggs and bury it so they will have it on their journeys back and forth across the desert.

There is some hunting of small animals. The Bushmen use spears, bow and arrow and sometimes chase game on foot.

The society is monogamous; it would be economically unsound for a man to have more than one wife since existence is precarious. The Bushman is a male-oriented society. The bands have chiefs who are descended from the fathers. Actually the chief is more a leader than a ruler. Their religion is supernatural with a great deal of emphasis upon the cult of the dead, in which the spirit of man stays with his people. The moon is the main deity, but stars are worshipped as well. Most prayers are for food. Rainfall is represented as a bull and is much feared and respected. The dancing of the band is elaborate and imitative of the animals the Bushmen hunt. A well developed art form once flourished and still may, as shown through many cave paintings, the most famous being the "White Lady of Brandberg" in South-West Africa.

HOTTENTOT

With a larger population than that of the Bushmen, the Hottentot are subdivided into tribes and have a more sound economic base. They are mainly located in South and South-West Africa. Chieftainships pass from father to son. The tribes are further divided into clans with the same male-descended leadership. Clan loyalty is stronger than tribal loyalty for the Hottentot is closer to the smaller organization. Like the Bushmen, the Hottentot were in the path of the Boer's northward expansion and suffered heavy losses in warfare and privation.

The Hottentot are primarily herdsmen raising cattle, goat and sheep, and are always searching for grazing ground. They stay longest at the large waterholes.

Unlike the Bushman society in which all property is communally owned, the Hottentot have private ownership of a parcel of land, but only by virtue of length of tenure. A newcomer must ask permission to share it. This permission is almost always granted. Homes and the equipment in them are private property and the unauthorized removal of any part of these is considered theft and is severely punished. There is some bartering in this society and an exchange of gifts such as Westerners practice. Inheritances are divided among the survivor's children. While the chiefs of the tribes and clans inherit their positions, they and the council must be approved by the group.

The Hottentot, like the Bushmen also worship the moon and, according to their folk-prayers, it promises the immortality of man. Dances are performed in celebration at the coming of each new moon. The Hottentot do not believe in an afterworld. They believe that a man's death is caused by man and not by supernatural means. The elderly are put out of their suffering by euthanasia; this also serves to hold the population in balance.

Bushmen quiver and arrows (left) are tools with which little nomads kill game for food. Arrowheads are dipped in poison. Forbidden to hunt in many areas, Bushmen youth (above) grow up accustomed to clothes and permanent shelters.

A contemporary Hottentot family (above) of father, mother and daughter. Below, a nineteenth century version of the Hottentot moon or harvest dance. Note the reeds used by dancers. Full moons are celebrated throughout the world.

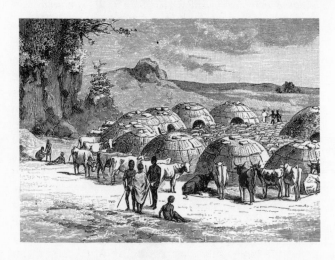

This Hottentot village (above), showing lambs enclosed and cattle outside, can be dismantled and moved as water and grazing lands are used up. Bare and somber, Griqualand West (top) is near the home of the Korana Hottentot region and Kimberley. A Pondo youth (right) looks over the Basutoland Reserve north of the East Hottentot region.

Makonde tribesmen dress in these costumes (above, right) for entertainment and the more important rituals, such as the boys coming of age. The march of the bride and groom (below) is repeated in many countries. Cattle given to bride's father is called "lobala" or "bridewealth." Above is Chief Marealle of the Chaggas, relative of Masai.

THE EAST AFRICAN CATTLE AREA

This area conforms roughly to the line of the Great Rift Valley; it is a corridor extending north and south from South Africa up through Kenya and into southern Egypt. A dual economy exists here of cattle herding and agriculture. Tribal and clan populations are numerous and therefore more complex than those of the Bushmen and Hottentot.

There is a little weaving from the bark of trees. Most of the clothing comes from the skins of animals. Families raise what they need in the way of food. There is no specialization of labor such as is found in West Africa. There are a few markets and bartering; money is not used except by the Europeans and the more urbanized African. In the south of this corridor, maize (corn) is plentiful and many diets are based on this. The cattle are used to buy brides and are termed "bridewealth." It is paid by the prospective husband to the father of the bride-to-be. A father with several daughters would probably gain many head of cattle.

Like the Hottentot, the local group commands more loyalty than the tribe or clan. Descent is counted down the father's side. There is some polygamy and, to offset it, exogamy or marriage outside one's group. This last protects against incest in the tightly knit local group and also maintains a balance in population. Secret societies have been undisclosed in East Africa, although the Mau-Mau uprisings in the 1950's indicated the possibilities.

In Kenya, "Ngai" is the highest god. This is not unlike other societies in East Africa where there is the definite concept of a single, high god with minor deities. On the other extreme are the natural (or nature) spirits and the ancestors. Religion is seldom discussed by tribal elders who know more about it than others. Magic, witchcraft and the workers of these are not always separated from religion.

The crest atop the head of this Batutsis native of Urundi (right) is typical of the region. The Batutsis may have come from northeast Africa 800 years ago. Pygmies are also found in Urundi near the Congo. Here women do housework and watch the child outside thatched hut (top). Typical of East African cattle complex are steer above.

THE CONGO REGION

The economy of this extremely large region is based on agriculture. (While many people work in the mines, etc., they do not get equal return for their labor and so agriculture remains basic.) The terrain prohibits the herding of any large domesticated animal. The farming staples are yams, maize, mullet and bananas. Fish is an important part of the diet. Chickens, goats and pigs are plentiful.

The Congo region was one hit most frequently by slave traders. When Leopold II of Belgium took it over as his private estate each district among the rubber plantations had to meet its quota or the hands of the workers were chopped off. With the encroachments of the slave traders and Leopold's ruthless terror the population fled into the interior to escape contact with the outside forces.

In the northeast section of the Congo region and in Gabon, wild game—such as elephants and lions—abounds. The natives have certain skills; there are iron workers, weavers, wood carvers, traders and hunters. While money is exchanged, it is generally considered the least important factor in trade; the barter system is preferred.

Before the onslaught of the Europeans many tribes had royal courts which ruled over vast kingdoms. Because the districts were so large, a system of local,

Bapende tribesmen of the Congo concealed in wooden masks and fibre jackets celebrate boys' coming of age (above). Deaths are mourned with different kinds of masks and drumming. Ivory craftsmen who hold positions of esteem in their tribes, work with special axes—the adze—and then polish ivory with wet leaves dipped in silica (below).

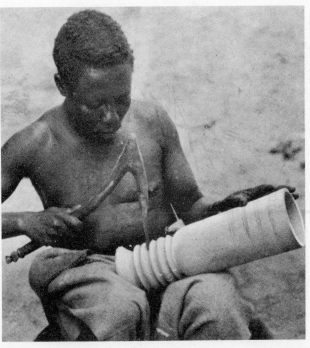

American Museum Journal

77

regional and higher courts were used to enforce the law. While the male ruler imposed his will over the populace all laws were subject to review by a council of elders.

Polygamy is found where the wealth and security permits it; usually it is the head man of a group or a chief of a tribe who is able to afford more than one wife. In religion, Mawa, the sun, is the female and the creator; Lesa, the moon, is male. Earth (Sagbata), thunder and rain (Henioso), and the sea (Age) are children of the two main gods. This concept is found with the Dahomey people and with certain variations in other tribes in the Guinea region. The Dahomey also worship snakes. The chief snake god, Da, is at once serpent, rainbow and umbilical cord.

In this region, on the bulge of West Africa, drumming with accompaniment from other instruments reaches a high degree of proficiency and complexity. In dancing, all parts of the body move but each section to the command of a distinct rhythm interwoven in the drumming or playing of other instruments.

Unrest in the Congo caused by political differences created a severe refugee problem in Elisabethville in 1962. A mother and her children seek shelter (left). A 19th century view of a pygmy at the Urundi border (below).

THE BAMBUTTI PYGMIES

In the gloom and tropic noise of the great Ituri forest in the Congo live the Bambutti (or Mbuti) pygmies. Few are over four feet tall. They appear in size at least to be related to the Bushmen of the Kalahari Desert. Also, like the Bushmen, they are nomadic and use poisoned weapons for hunting. The pygmies are quite friendly.

Pygmy groups living in the Congo region have local village autonomy. Sometimes the small people serve as feudal-like serfs to the members of tribes taller than themselves. While this arrangement is based on fear, when the pygmies become enraged the taller people scatter; the poisoned arrow of the pygmy is greatly respected. They use swing ropes to cross rivers they either cannot swim or boat across. They seldom have possession of craft for travelling over bodies of water. It is not known whether the rule of the pygmy comes from the patriarchal or matriarchal side. Having no agriculture, the little people have both hunters and food gatherers.

Little is known of pygmy religions. Throughout the Congo area the idea of one high god continues. "Nzambe," or variations of this, is the name of that god. Other deities continue the idea of man related to the spirits of his ancestors.

THE GUINEA COAST AREA

The last in the five major living areas below the Sahara, the Guinea Coast has the greatest population density. It has the most complex division of labor, religion and art. While the tribal line still remains, sub-groupings and a western-style family set-up are more prevalent. This is especially true in the larger cities of the independent nations which must have contact with the outside in order to bring about the full fruition of a free state. Here the division of labor is highly specialized, for there are many diverse industrial possibilities, some of which are already underway and some have been in process for centuries—such as gold mining and metal-casting.

Because of the tsetse fly, there are few cattle in this region. In addition there are few plains for animal grazing. However, goats and sheep are seen in the northern parts and chickens are maintained in both northern and southern areas. Rice, cocoa, cassava, maize and palm products provide the backbone of agricultural products. Both men and women prepare the ground for crops in perhaps the only shared division of labor. (Women cannot play the drums.)

National Geographical Society

Kano, Moslem mud city in northern Nigeria (above), was center for Songhai Empire. Life near here traced to 4000 B.C. A Dahomey warrior stands in old battle dress (right). Two hoes used for ages by West African farmers (below).

Mercaldo Archives

There are wood carvers, home builders and pottery makers. Brass makers hold prestige positions. Guilds in this area serve as price-fixing councils. Iron workers have their own subdivisions: smelters, pourers, etc. There are also cloth weavers some of whom make the famous kente cloth worn by many people in the Guinea Coast region. Some kente robes cost upwards of $300 and are draped over shoulders and body as with the Indian shari.

While some money changes hands among the more westernized and therefore urbanized peoples, the cowrie shell is still in great use as the basic currency. The cowrie shell is from a small marine animal and has a high gloss. It is also used as money in some parts of Asia.

Family succession is in most cases patriarchal.

Peul women from Upper Volta (left) wear distinctive head-dresses and carry children in body slings. The adinkira cloth (below) traditionally used in the making of the Ghanaian kente has become popular in the West. Fetishes (below, left) are endowed with many qualities, one of the more important being fertility; another was power or wisdom.

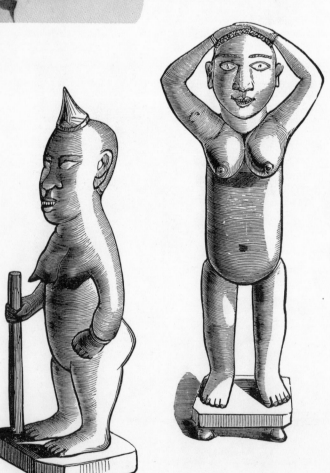

Ghana Information Service

80

United Nations

Dahomeyan drum-makers (left) test their instruments. In West Africa each ceremony requires a special drum. Using the aluminal thermite process a Gabon workman welds a railhead (above). A pottery maker near Hohoe, Togoland, plies his trade (below, left). These people depend on small-scale agriculture and trading for livelihood; south Togo is more prosperous than north. An Abuakwa, Ghana, family pounds Foufou dough, a starch, into shape (below).

United Nations

UNICEF Photo by Paul Almasy

Banana people live in houses built on stilts near Yaounde, Cameroons (left). Malaria control units have been set up here. Marketing is generally handled by women in West Africa. In a village near Lomé, Togoland, a woman strides away with her goods on her head (below, left). The Tiko Banana Plantation in the Cameroons (above) is one of the major exporters of the fruit. Below, a young Guinean girl.

The old and the new merge in the capital of Egypt, Cairo. Shown here (above) is the entrance to the Mowsky bazaar. Although Arab nomads are moving to the cities, many still prefer to live as their ancestors (above, right) on the fringes of the desert. This Kabyle woman of Algeria stands in ceremonial dress (right). The Kabyle are Berbers and reside in Tunisia and Algeria. They speak Berber dialects.

NORTH AFRICA

The vast top of Africa running from the Atlantic Ocean to the Red Sea is generally regarded as the land of Allah, for the Mohammedan religion has deep roots here and they extend down into the northernmost fringes of tropical Africa. Because of the desert, the populations are ringed around the Mediterranean seacoast. The division of labor is extensive and complex—fishing, sailing, merchandising (or trading). Both money and objects are used as purchasing currency. Centuries of contact with Europe have just about established a pattern of monogamy, although there are many cases of multiple marriages and harems. The discovery of petroleum and other minerals has increased the specialization of labor, since many who are native to these regions have been pressed into these industries.

A scarcity of rain makes life difficult for those who live in or on the fringes of the Sahara. These are nomads and have lived in this manner for generations roaming back and forth across the desert, herding sometimes goats and chickens which seem to be able to survive the rigors of life in this region. The societies in the north are male-oriented. Of late, the patterns of living for those in the desert regions have been disrupted by the French testing of atomic weapons.

A street vendor selling his wares in the "Souk" section of Morocco (above, left). Near the Garian-Tripoli road, a young farmer uses a camel to plough dry Libyan earth (above). In extreme rural areas methods of farming have not changed in generations. The Tuareg tribes (below) belong to three main groups: Asgars, Haggars and Kelowais.

THE TUAREG

It has been true that the Tuareg men wear veils; that their faces are never left uncovered. Now, just as the veils are being dropped from the faces of many women in North Africa who are Mohammedans, so it is true that the Tuareg can sometimes be found with dropped veil. The Tuareg live deep in the Sahara or along the tops of the Niger and Mali republics. While they use fleet Arabian horses, they also ride the mehari racing camel, usually white in color and sleek in appearance. In full dress the Tuareg also wear a long, medieval-looking sword. They were once the scourge of the Sahara, raiding the caravans, plundering and often killing. Like many other people in Africa, the Tuareg are a mixture of many different stocks, but are generally of the Mohammedan faith.

CREATIVE AFRICA

British Museum

Ife memorial head (top, right) resembles one found by Frobenius in Nigeria in 1910. Ife craftsmen preceded the Beni. Cast bronze vessels were made by the Ashanti of Ghana as well as the Beni. This one (above) held powder.

ART

In the absence of written language below the Sahara the art of the people in these regions has had to be the great voice. This art is almost always confined to sculpture. While there are many utilitarian works of art, tools and vessels, for example, those pieces of art which serve no function other than to establish communication with nature are to the African himself art.

The pyramids, temples, statues and obelisks of the Nile Valley while exciting and monumental examples of art are only a part of the colorful and varied artistic African gold mine. Much of the art—that of architecture and cave painting such as is found in Zimbabwe in Southern Rhodesia and in South-West Africa, respectively—is enveloped in mystery. Who, for example, painted the "White Lady of Brandberg" which is so Grecian in aspect? What people built the Zimbabwe complex—and then vanished?

No one yet knows.

It is known, however, that the sculpture of Africa is almost totally derived from the two great river systems of the Congo and Niger in West and Central Africa. The sculpture which so vastly influenced European artists in the early 1900's came from these regions. Among the artists who saw magnificent styling and fusion of man and nature were Picasso, Braque and Modigliani. They began a new school of painting highlighted by "Cubism," which seemed the basis for Afri-

can sculpture. The "distortions" in African sculpture led the Cubists to realize that the sculpture was designed through mathematical proportioning, or bending the emotional responses to the hard demand of nature.

African art is highly collectivistic and not individualistic as is western art. The African artist is concerned with the total experiences of his tribe or clan and all his ancestors. He is concerned with what is good or what is bad in nature.

Animism—the endowing of inanimate objects with power—is not confined to African sculpture below the Sahara. Babylonians, Greeks, Romans, Teutons, Egyptians—indeed many people practiced it. We have animism today in various religions, advertising and so on.

Magic—black and white—the first designed to prevent harm, the second to encourage good luck, was involved in the art along with tribal religion and mythology. Since life was hard and deaths were many, fertility statuaries were quite prominent. Many dance masks have found their way into western museums. The masks were worn to celebrate harvests, for religious or political functions and for various society gatherings. Since a few animals were thought to have god-like powers, there is statuary devoted to them.

Stone, wood, ivory, brass, bronze, gold and copper were and still are the materials of the African sculptor. The adze, the woodcarver's tool, is used as a mallet, chisel or knife. The favorite wood is iroko because it cuts like soft wood and then hardens.

Soapstone is preferred by stonecutters and sculpture of this material has been found in the Kalahari desert and in mysterious Zimbabwe.

The medieval metal-caster of the Benue Valley in Nigeria used wax or wild rubber for the "master" of his sculpture. Then bronze or another pliable metal was conducted through vents into the "master." Only the West African countries have produced sculpture by this method called the *cire perdue* or lost wax.

Albert Barnes, an American collector, established one of the first museums in America for African art. William Fagg, Deputy Keeper of the Department of Ethnology of the British Museum, was also instrumental in focusing attention on African sculpture.

The independence of many African nations has increased the price of art objects. On the other hand, many of these nations have closed their borders against collectors and are trying to buy back the pieces taken from their country. The sculpture now in circulation is rarely more than three hundred years old.

Top to bottom: *Ceremonial mask of the Mano in Liberia; very likely a mask made upon the death of the tribesman. Another Ashanti bronze vessel; the Ashanti were also gold workers, specializing in weights. Fertility figures, important in nearly all of Africa, are sometimes half-sized such as this one from the Pangwe, Gabon. The Beni craftsmen were perhaps truer to life than the Ife, as this head reveals. Baluba produced this female figure with stool.*

(1)

(3)

(2)

(4)

British Museum

British Museum

Collection of the Smith College Museum of Art

American Museum Journal

(5)

United Nations

(6)

Helmet mask of wood worn by the Bamum of Cameroons
(1). Baluba carvers created ceremonial axe designed for head
fighting only (2). The Ife royal figures are kings in the
succession to the throne ritual (3). Mangbetu of the
Congo carved figures on jars and vessels (4). Two Suah Dua
or "ju-ju" men and village life are brass-castings by the
lost-wax process (5). The highly stylized female mask is
Bapende and the bold, almost Gothic one is Yoruba (6).
Modigliani's Stone Head marks a strong African influence (7).

(7)

This Malinke dance was captured by a 19th century artist visiting West Africa (top). From the same period a Balunda playing the marimba and a few of the many drums, harp and pipes of West African musicians (above). Guinea boys perform ritualistic dance with bells on their feet (below).

DANCING

Dancing became an art in the west. For the African it was always purely functional; he danced for rain, for a good harvest, for healthy children and for joy. Women were banned from the majority of dances. In the western cultures dancing became an emotional and erotic act and had little function in nature.

LITERATURE

In the Nile Valley the literature first concerned the gods. Originally it was not set down but passed verbally from generation to generation, changing as it went. Then the literature could be written in hieroglyphics upon papyrus. These told of the exploits of great kings and armies and battles. Below the Sahara the literature, with few exceptions, was verbal and also passed from generation to generation. This was mostly ritualistic literature. When it was not, it was legend or folk tale, often embodying animals as central characters. While on the surface this aspect of literature might have seemed amusing, it was really extremely moral and taught lessons in human behavior, in the manner of Aesop.

Some of the battle songs of the Zulu show great complexity and beauty in translation though some translations are inaccurate and consequently whatever strength lay in the original tongue is now lost.

Africa will in time present the world with its literature. Leopold Sedar Senghor, President of the Republic of Senegal, who writes in French is an accomplished poet and essayist. He leads a host of younger writers from all over the continent.

MUSIC

The music of Africa below (and to a large extent above) the Sahara has always been based largely on rhythm, followed closely by harmony and last, if at all, by melody. This is just the opposite of popular music in America and the west where melody is most important, harmony next and rhythm last.

The African slaves are believed to have brought with them to the new world the rhythms which are the basis of jazz, a genre of American popular music.

From the beginning, however, jazz contained European influences and was seldom of pure African origin. Closer to the intricate and sophisticated rhythms of Africa are those found in South and Caribbean America. Even here some European influences, particularly Spanish, have been felt. There are isolated villages where the rhythm and harmony have remained more African than European.

Among vocal music, remnants of the West African call and response chants are still to be found in the American Deep South. These were once very prominent because they were used in the singing of spirituals which, although they were not native to the earliest African slaves, were adopted by them but sung as their ancestors had sung chants.

AN AFRICAN
FACTFINDER

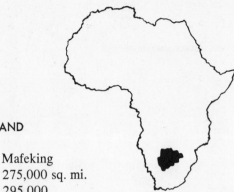

BECHUANALAND

Capital: Mafeking
Area: 275,000 sq. mi.
Population: 295,000

Bechuanaland is a British protectorate located in South Central Africa between the Union of South Africa, South-West Africa, and Southern Rhodesia. Bechuanaland is on a plateau 3,000 ft. high. Cattle raising and dairy farming are main occupations of this region which came under British control in 1885. Bushmen and Bantu language people, Asians and whites live here. Lion, rhinoceros, hippopotamuses, giraffe, antelopes, gazelles and leopards are common. There is one mining district, Francistown, where gold and silver are obtained.

Giraffes take flight in foliage of Bechuanaland (above).

South Africa

BASUTOLAND

Capital: Maseru
Area: 11,716 sq. mi.
Population: 578,000

Basutoland is a colony of Great Britain, surrounded by the Union of South Africa. It became a native state in 1843 under a treaty signed with chief Moshesh. Sheep and cattle raising are the main industries. Basutoland is for all intents and purposes a native reserve, for few white men are allowed on this land of the Basuto people. Climate is dry, ranging from a low of ten degrees to a high of ninety-five. Annual rainfall is thirty inches.

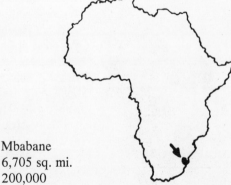

SWAZILAND

Capital: Mbabane
Area: 6,705 sq. mi.
Population: 200,000

Swaziland is a British protectorate lying at the southeastern end of the Transvaal. Under British protection since 1900, cattle raising is a chief occupation. Tin, gold and asbestos are her main exports. Wild game, similar to that in Bechuanaland, is found here. The mean temperature is sixty-two degrees. Rainfall varies from twenty to forty inches annually. The native population is composed of Zulus who speak Swazi and Zulu.

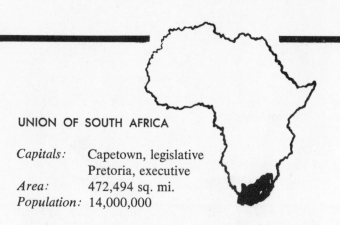

UNION OF SOUTH AFRICA

Capitals: Capetown, legislative
Pretoria, executive
Area: 472,494 sq. mi.
Population: 14,000,000

Leader: Prime Minister Hendrik F. Verwoerd

Union of South Africa is an independent state and until 1961 a member of the British Commonwealth of Nations. She gained independence in 1910, nine years after the Boer War. Lying at the southern tip of Africa with almost 70 per cent of her population African, South Africa's policy of Apartheid (segregation) has caused her to be rebuffed by most members of the Commonwealth, which was the reason she withdrew in 1961. Frequent and violent race riots and

continued oppression of all the non-white majority have severely undermined South Africa's potential as a vital nation. Sheep and cattle raising are prominent and ostrich raising was once very important. Gold is mined in profusion but South Africa's greatest wealth lies in her diamond mines, the largest in the world.

Hendrik F. Verwoerd (top) is the prime minister of Union of South Africa. Cape Peninsula (center) is its southernmost part and the springhok (right) its symbol. Ostrich farming (above) is plentiful. Opposite page: Kruger National Park has 900 lions, 400 leopards, 1,000 elephants, 2,000 giraffes, 2,500 wart hogs, 2,600 hippopotami, 7,800 buffaloes, 7,800 wildbeests, 8,000 zebras and over 100,000 antelopes. Many laborers (top, right) are brought from Mozambique at low wages. Bottom of page are an Afrikander stub bull and Johannesburg, founded with discovery of gold.

South African Railways

FEDERATION OF RHODESIA AND NYASALAND

NORTHERN RHODESIA

Prime Minister: Sir Roy Welensky

Capital: Lusaka
Area: 290,320 sq. mi.
Population: 1,977,000

SOUTHERN RHODESIA

Capital: Salisbury
Area: 150,354 sq. mi.
Population: 2,233,000

NYASALAND

Capital: Zomba
Area: 48,444 sq. mi.
Population: 2,401,000

National Geographical Society

Sir Roy Welensky (top) is the prime minister of Federation of Rhodesia and Nyasaland. The above mine lies in the Northern Rhodesia copper belt. Kenneth Kaunda (right) and Dr. Hastings Banda (below, right) are Nationalist leaders in Northern Rhodesia and Nyasaland, respectively. Salisbury, pictured below, is the capital of Southern Rhodesia.

Federal Information Department, Southern Rhodesia

Northern Rhodesia and *Nyasaland* are British protectorates annexed in 1924 and 1891, respectively, while *Southern Rhodesia* is a self-governing British colony annexed in 1923. All three have been involved in a federation which, to say the least, has been troublesome and at times unworkable. Together the chief products are: tobacco, maize, wheat, tea, cotton and peanuts. Minerals are copper, cobalt, vanadium, lead, zinc, asbestos, gold, coal, bauxite and chrome ore. Cattle and sheep raising are also prominent. These territories are set on a plateau; Nyasaland has a highland similar to Kenya's. The rainy season exists from November to March, the annual rainfall running between twenty and sixty inches. David Livingstone made his discoveries and many Christian converts among the Africans at Zomba, the capital of Nyasaland.

Dr. Hastings Banda and Kenneth Kuanda are the popular voices of the peoples of Nyasaland and Northern Rhodesia.

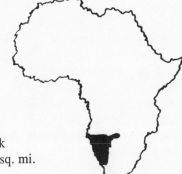

SOUTH-WEST AFRICA

Capital: Windhoek
Area: 317,725 sq. mi.
Population: 424,000

South-West Africa became a mandate of the Union of South Africa following World War I. It is now a trust territory administered by the Union under United Nations supervision. Like Bechuanaland and South Africa, South-West Africa is touched by the Kalahari Desert. Another great desert, the Namib, traverses South-West Africa in the North. The plateau, a part of that great land mass upon which also rests the Union of South Africa, ranges from 3,000 to about 8,000 feet.

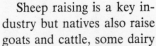

Sheep raising is a key industry but natives also raise goats and cattle, some dairy production and great amounts of wheat and corn. Minerals include diamonds, gold, vanadium, tungsten, lead, tin, iron ore and copper. The coast line is rich with sea foods. Seals frequent the beaches in great numbers. Rainfall sometimes is less than an inch per year. South-West Africa's close relationship with the Union of South Africa has not improved tensions between black and white Africans.

Wankie coal mine (above) is located in Southern Rhodesia. Tobacco is one of Southern Rhodesia's most important exports. The scene below is of a tobacco auction in Salisbury.

United Nations

The Rehoboth school children (above) are of mixed descent. Manatee (below) are found along Africa's south-west coast.

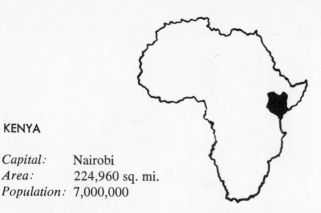

East Africa

KENYA

Capital: Nairobi
Area: 224,960 sq. mi.
Population: 7,000,000

Kenya is both a colony and protectorate of Great Britain. Held by the Imperial British East Africa Company from 1888-1905, she became a crown colony in 1920. Sitting on a plateau which ranges to above 9,000 feet, Kenya is at once tropical, sub-tropical and temperate. The Highlands, the most pleasant area of the country, is restricted to whites.

A variety of crops are grown here where the earliest of sailors and explorers from the east came. Safaris usually move into Kenya and neighboring Tanganyika for the big game which is rapidly being depleted. Game preserves and tight supervision of hunting have helped, but not enough. Kenya is the home of Mount Kenya (17,040 feet), an extinct volcano whose slopes carry the weight of a dozen or more glaciers.

Her chief minerals are gold, sodium carbonate, silver and salt. Sisal, meat, tea and coffee are her agricultural products for export. More than forty varieties of snakes have been found in Kenya. There are two rainy seasons: April, May and June and the second in October, November and December. These occur at the time of the monsoons which for hundreds of years plagued eastern sailors. Temperature range is from thirty-five up to ninety degrees.

Independence is expected in the very near future. Tom Mboya is an outstanding political leader of Kenya.

United Nations

Top sketches show a spotted hyena (left) and a python swallowing a bird (right); both are typical of Kenya. At center is an eland herd; above is the Nairobi airfield.

94

THE MASAI

It is said of the Masai, who live on the southern border of Kenya, that they are so brave they may dress and adorn themselves in what might to a foreigner appear a feminine fashion. The Masai hunt lion with nothing except spear and shield. They too count their wealth in cattle but never kill them for food, though they will drink the blood.

TANGANYIKA

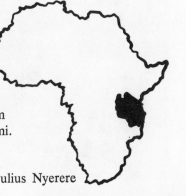

Capital: Dar-es-Salaam
Area: 362,688 sq. mi.
Population: 9,404,000

Leader: President-Elect Julius Nyerere

Tanganyika along with Rwanda-Urundi made up German East Africa from 1884 until 1919. It was then administered under a League of Nations mandate by Great Britain and became a United Nations trust territory still under Great Britain in 1948. Mount Kilimanjaro (19,565 ft.) is the highest mountain on the continent. Even though below the Equator snow remains on the peaks all year. Tanganyika has the same problem with depletion of big game as Kenya. One of the game preserves is on the

United Nations

Above is a new hospital at Dar es Salaam, the capital of Tanganyika. Center sketches outline the dreaded tsetse fly.

Serengetti Plains.

Like Kenya, Tanganyika's greatest export products are sisal, coffee and tea. In addition she exports cotton. Peanuts and sugar cane are also big crops. Cattle, goat and sheep herds are numerous. Tanganyika also possesses gold and diamonds, silver, tin and tungsten. From her ample forests come timber, gum arabic, copal and beeswax. She rests upon a great table land which sometimes rises to over 8,000 feet. Two rainy seasons prevail here also. Because there is little jungle in Tanganyika and mostly vast plains, it is often called Blue Africa because one can see over long distances without obstruction; this causes everything in the distance to appear blue.

Tanganyika became independent December 28, 1961. She is a member of the British Commonwealth.

95

Among the animals of Tanganyika are the oryx (top, left), the zebra (above, left) and the adjutant stork (above). The motto of its official coat-of-arms (top) is "Freedom and Unity." To the left is a baobab tree and below is a part of the monthly shipment of 20,000 tons of sisal.

United Nations

Above is the U. N. Technical Assistance Office at Tanarive, Malagasy; below, President Philibert Tsiranana. At left are a Swahili family of Malagasy and women pounding rice.

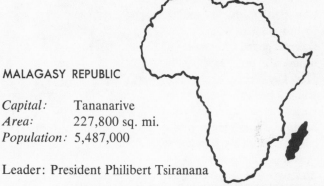

MALAGASY REPUBLIC

Capital: Tananarive
Area: 227,800 sq. mi.
Population: 5,487,000

Leader: President Philibert Tsiranana

Malagasy (previously Madagascar), a former French colony, gained its independence in 1960. It is an island almost as large as Mozambique and is 250 miles wide. Population is a mixture of Micronesian and Polynesian people who probably arrived there in great outrigger canoes from Oceania; there are Africans as well. Malagasy came under French protection in 1885 and became a colony in 1896. There seems to have been a succession of queens rather than kings on the island. Her forests provide gum, medicinal plants, rubber, tannis and dyewoods. Tobacco, cloves, sugar, coffee, vanilla, maize, coconuts and rice are among her main crops. Her minerals are gold, mica and phosphates. A plateau, Malagasy has a great variety of wild life and many kinds of livestock. The town of Antsirabé, a health resort, has some of the finest curative hot springs in the world.

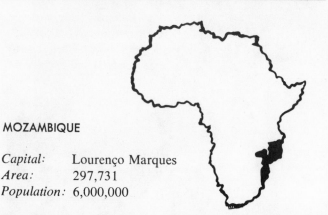

MOZAMBIQUE

Capital: Lourenço Marques
Area: 297,731
Population: 6,000,000

Mozambique, more than ten times the size of Portugal and considered by that nation to be but an overseas extension or province of the mainland, stretches for more than 1400 miles along the Mozambique Channel, a section of the Indian Ocean. Cotton, sugar, copra, cashew nuts and tea are main crops. Her minerals are gold, coal, graphite and mica. Recent disclosures have indicated that the Portuguese have exceeded even the Union of South Africa in oppressing the black African population. In fact, Mozambique and South African officials have a working agreement whereby the workers in the mines of South Africa are shipped from across the border in Mozambique to work in virtual slavery. The chief seaport of Mozambique, Beira, in addition to shipping out its own wealth also handles that of Katanga in what was formerly the Belgian Congo. Annual rainfall is about thirty-seven inches and the usual temperature is around seventy-five.

ETHIOPIA

Capital: Addis Ababa
Area: 350,000 sq. mi.
Population: 20,000,000 (est.)

Leader: Emperor Haile Selassie

ERITREA

Capital: Asmara
Area: 45,754 sq. mi.
Population: over 1,000,000

United Nations

N. Y. Public Library, Picture Collection

Ethiopia, the African stronghold of the Coptic Christian faith, is mainly upon a plateau where cattle, sheep, goats, horses and mules are bred extensively. Her key crops are maize, wheat, barley, rye, cotton, sugar cane, millet and hemp. The temperature range is from sixty to eighty degrees. There are two dry and two wet seasons. Ethiopia has for generations been an independent kingdom, but suffered occupation by Italian forces from 1936 to 1941.

Eritrea is federated with Ethiopia. Like most countries in the cattle complex, Eritrea is rich in livestock. Salt mining is one of the most important industries. She also produces gold and potassium salts. Many of the world's pearls come from her seacoast waters. A base for the American forces during World War II, Eritrea was once held by the Italians. Her average temperature is eighty-six degrees but pushes up to one hundred and twenty.

Pictured above is Ethiopia's Emperor Haile Selassie. Below are a native of Ethiopia and the obelisk at Axum, ancient seat of Ethiopian power. Addis Ababa, the capital of Ethiopia, is at the lower, right-hand corner. At the top is the Mosque of Koren in Eritrea and, to the right, is the black-face sheep, important to that country's economy.

Ethiopian Airlines

Mercaldo Archives

Ethiopian Airlines

Ships of this type (above), called dhows, carry cloves from Zanzibar, the clove center of the world, to India. At right we see a typical Zanzibar Arab family. Aden Abdulla Osman (below) is the president of Somalia. Bananas (below, right) grown in irrigated Genalle region are a principal Somalia export. Below, right, are a Somali man and woman and (bottom of page) Mogadiscio, the capital of Somalia.

ZANZIBAR and PEMBA

Capital: Zanzibar
Area: 1,020 sq. mi.
Population: 275,000

Zanzibar and *Pemba*, two islands off the coast of Tanganyika, are British protectorates, having had that status since 1890. Famous for cloves, clove and coconut oil and copra, the islands furnish the world with about eighty per cent of its cloves. They are subject to the gusts of the monsoons, which occur twice a year.

Independence, although no date has been set, has been agreed upon.

SOMALIA

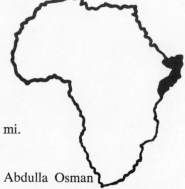

Capital: Mogadiscio
Area: 246,000 sq. mi.
Population: 2,000,000

Leader: President Aden Abdulla Osman

Somalia (Italian Somaliland) was once divided between the British (1884) and the Italians (1889) but in 1960 became a single independent country. Since the country has a great many cattle, hides are one of her chief exports. Her sparse forests yield gums and resins. Bananas, cotton and spices round out the inventory of her products. There is some limited mining of tin which bolsters an otherwise slender economy. It is subject to both dry spells and monsoons.

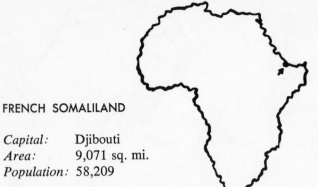

FRENCH SOMALILAND

Capital: Djibouti
Area: 9,071 sq. mi.
Population: 58,209

French Somaliland is considered an overseas French territory. It adjoins Somalia to the east and like it has a great many cattle. Her chief mineral is salt. The climate is quite dry and hot, the monsoon seasons notwithstanding.

At right is the manioc or cassava plant of French Somaliland and, top of page, the secretary vulture, also of this area.

SENEGAL

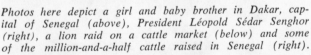

Capital: St.-Louis
Area: 76,000 sq. mi.
Population: 2,973,000

Leader: President Léopold Sédar Senghor

Permanent Mission of Senegal to U. N.

Photos here depict a girl and baby brother in Dakar, capital of Senegal (above), President Léopold Sédar Senghor (right), a lion raid on a cattle market (below) and some of the million-and-a-half cattle raised in Senegal (right).

Senegal was the home of the first slaves brought to America. Dakar, a seaport, has been known to sailors for centuries. The rainy season is from May to October; the mean temperature is eighty-two degrees. Rubber, palm products, ground (g'ru)nuts, bananas and pineapples are chief agricultural products. Phospates are the country's sole mineral. Cattle and sheep are raised on the Fouta Djallon Plateau, inhabited mostly by Fulani.

Independent since 1960, Senegal was a former French territory. With Dahomey, Sudan and Upper (Haute) Volta, she made the beginnings of a federation (the Mali Federation) but still within the French community. Senegal is considered an autonomous republic.

GUINEA

Capital: Conakry
Area: 95,000 sq. mi.
Population: 2,900,000

Leader: President Sékou Touré

West Africa —

Embassy of Guinea to the U. S.

Guinea left the French family of nations in September, 1958, voting not to remain as other African nations had within the French Union. She since formed a loose alliance with Ghana and an even looser one with Liberia. Her chief products are coffee, fruit and bauxite. Her forests and minerals are largely undeveloped. The harmattan, a hot dust-filled wind, blows over this section of Africa from November to April.

Sékou Touré (top) is the president of Guinea. Above is some of its wildlife and below, yams, one of its products.

GAMBIA

Capital: Bathurst
Area: 4,005 sq. mi.
Population: 280,000

Leader: President D. K. Jawara

Gambia is a British colony and protectorate that lies in a ten-mile-wide strip on both sides of the Gambia River. She became a colony in 1843. Her main export is the peanut or ground nut. Livestock are raised and there are some palm products. The temperature range is from fifty-six to one hundred and sixty-five degrees.

101

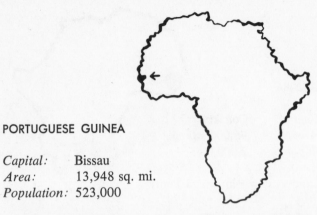

PORTUGUESE GUINEA

Capital: Bissau
Area: 13,948 sq. mi.
Population: 523,000

Portuguese Guinea has been a colony since 1879. Mostly undeveloped, her chief export is the peanut. Other products are coconuts, ivory, palm products and rice. Timber, wax and rubber come from her forests. The annual rainfall is well over sixty inches. United States President Ulysses S. Grant served as mediator in a dispute between Great Britain and Portugal for the possession of Guinea. He judged that Portugal was the rightful owner.

Government Information Services, Sierra Leone

Sierra Leone has highly productive iron-ore mines (below) and produces the commercial kola nut (bottom). Sir Milton Margai is its prime minister (bottom, left). Above are the Kama Kowei dancers and left center, the great seal.

Government Information Services, Sierra Leone

SIERRA LEONE

Capital: Freetown
Area: 27,924 sq. mi.
Population: 2,600,000

Leader: Prime Minister Sir Milton Margai

Sierra Leone, one of the most highly developed countries in West Africa, became independent early in 1961 after being a British colony and protectorate since 1896. Diamond-rich, the country also has gold, platinum and iron ore, with extremely high metal content, as chief minerals. Her agricultural products are varied: palm products, rubber, millet, cassava, cocoa, coffee, ginger and rice. There are also a great number of kola nut and mangrove trees. Freetown, one of the best harbors in West Africa, was a natural and strategic base for the Allied forces during World War II. Average annual rainfall is over sixty inches.

Sierra Leone is a British Commonwealth member.

102

Liberian Information Service

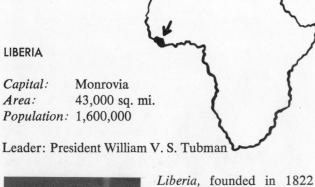

LIBERIA

Capital: Monrovia
Area: 43,000 sq. mi.
Population: 1,600,000

Leader: President William V. S. Tubman

United Nations

Liberia, founded in 1822 by returned American slaves similar to the founding of Freetown for British slaves and ex-servicemen, became the first African republic in 1847. With an average annual rainfall upwards of sixty inches, Liberia has excellent rubber forests which are worked by the Firestone Rubber Company of the United States. Diamond, gold, copper and zinc mines are now under development.

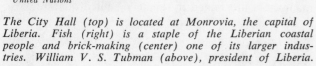

The City Hall (top) is located at Monrovia, the capital of Liberia. Fish (right) is a staple of the Liberian coastal people and brick-making (center) one of its larger industries. William V. S. Tubman (above), president of Liberia.

IVORY COAST

Capital: Abidjan
Area: 125,000 sq. mi.
Population: 3,300,000

Leader: Premier Félix Houphouet-Boigny

Ivory Coast, an autonomous republic within the French community since 1960, was formerly a section of the colony of French West Africa dating from 1893. This part of West Africa and the adjoining sections were frequently called "the grain coast" because of the varieties of grain found here. The chief exports are lumber (an unusually excellent mahogany) and coffee (the world's third largest producer). Like other west coast countries, the Ivory Coast has two dry seasons —December to March, and August and September. Rain generally prevails at other times, reaching a measurement of over seven feet per year. Palm products, cocoa, bananas and cotton are also important in this region which got its name because of the elephant tusks obtained here. The elephants have either moved further south or have been all but exterminated. Gold and manganese are mined in severely limited quantities.

Félix Houphouet-Boigny (above) is president of Ivory Coast. Gorillas (left) are still found in great number though the elephant (top) is very nearly extinct in this region.

104

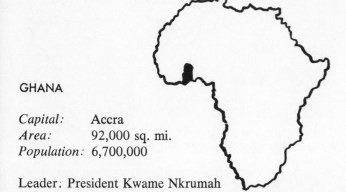

GHANA

Capital: Accra
Area: 92,000 sq. mi.
Population: 6,700,000

Leader: President Kwame Nkrumah

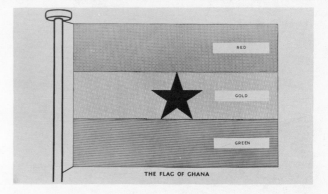

RED

GOLD

GREEN

THE FLAG OF GHANA

Ghana, named for an ancient African empire north of the present republic, was known as the Gold Coast. Ghana supplies the world with more than a third of its cocoa. Wood, diamonds, gold and manganese ore are her chief export products. She is also just beginning to exploit her vast deposits of bauxite. Ghana led the parade for independence below the Sahara in March, 1957. She has, however, remained within the British Commonwealth of Nations. Takoradi, a seaport, was the starting point for the delivery of British aircraft to Egypt during World War II. Ghana has an average temperature of eighty degrees, which seems higher because of the humidity.

FREEDOM JUSTICE AND

Partially through her world commerce in cocoa (top, left) Ghana has been able to modernize—a new bridge spans an old river (top, right). Above are Ghana's flag and seal.

TOGO

Capital: Lome
Area: 19,000 sq. mi.
Population: 1,440,000

Leader: President Sylvanus Olympio

Togo(land), an autonomous republic, has seen British, German and French rule. A German colony from 1884, she was under a League of Nations mandate following World War I with Britain in control of one third of it and the French administering the rest. Togo became a United Nations trust territory in 1946 and independent of European rule in 1960. Like Ghana her chief crop is cocoa. Chimpanzee, leopard, buffalo and crocodile are common here as in Ghana and the Ivory Coast. Palm products, cotton and copra are important agricultural items. Togo mines iron ore and her forests give dyewoods. Heavy rains of the monsoon type and the stiff, dry harmattan winds provide the chief climatic changes. The rainfall averages sixty inches a year.

Togolese children attend the Mawuli school (top). Chimpanzee (left) are common and the oil palm tree affords a great profit. At center of page is President Sylvanus Olympio.

DAHOMEY

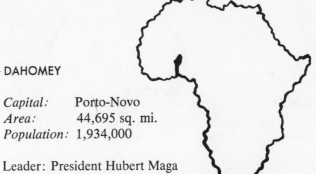

Capital: Porto-Novo
Area: 44,695 sq. mi.
Population: 1,934,000

Leader: President Hubert Maga

Dahomey once had an Amazon warrior force which had the place of honor in any battle; the ladies of the tribe acquitted themselves well. Dahomey was annexed by the French in 1894. She became independent in 1960. No minerals are mined here, though they have been located. When developed the Dahomey plains will yield iron, bauxite and kaolin. For the moment at least cotton, peanuts and rubber bring the most revenue. Porto-Novo and Cotonou are the chief cities of the nation.

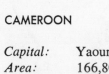

CAMEROON

Capital: Yaoundé
Area: 166,800 sq. mi.
Population: 4,907,000

Leader: President Ahmadou Ahidjo

Cameroon like Togo has seen German, British and French rule. A former colony of Germany until the end of World War I, it was shared by the British and French until after World War II when she became a United Nations trust territory of France. She obtained her independence on January 1, 1960. Cameroon produces coffee, cocoa, bananas, aluminum and palm products. Rainfall exceeds sixty inches annually. Malaria is prevalent.

Ruling the republics of Dahomey and Cameroon are President Hubert Maga (above) and President Ahmadou Ahidjo (below, left). Children (below) study in a Cameroon schoolroom.

United Nations

GABON

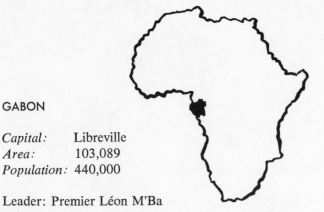

Capital: Libreville
Area: 103,089
Population: 440,000

Leader: Premier Léon M'Ba

Gabon is the richest and smallest of the four countries (Gabon, Congo Republic, Chad and Central African Republic) which once made up French Equatorial Africa. Chief products are oil, iron, manganese, timber, cocoa and gold. Libreville became the home of Africans freed from slave ships in 1842.

CONGO REPUBLIC

Capital: Brazzaville
Area: 132,046 sq. mi.
Population: 900,000

Leader: President Fulbert Youlou

Congo Republic is for the most part covered with dense tropical forests. Its main resources are lumber, peanuts and palm oil.

United Nations

Léon M'Ba (top, left) is premier of Gabon; top, right, is a typical Gabon village. As tropical trees are cut down a new skyscraper goes up in Brazzaville (left), the capital of Congo Republic; above is its president, Fulbert Youlou.

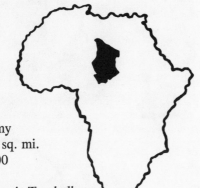

CHAD

Capital: Fort-Lamy
Area: 495,752 sq. mi.
Population: 2,675,000

Leader: Premier François Tombalbaye

Chad is an arid, landlocked country. Livestock, fish, cotton, rice and peanuts are important products. Lead, tin, copper and diamonds have been found in each of these three countries.

Shown here are the leaders of Chad and Central African Republic: Premier François Tombalbaye (right) and President David Dacko (below, right). Below, a young woman of the Republic and (bottom) workers in the cotton fields.

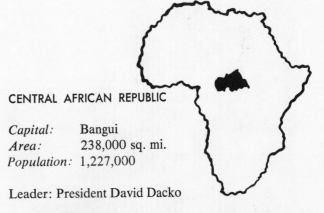

CENTRAL AFRICAN REPUBLIC

Capital: Bangui
Area: 238,000 sq. mi.
Population: 1,227,000

Leader: President David Dacko

Central African Republic is also landlocked. Cotton, coffee, peanuts, timber and some diamonds are the base of her products.

These four countries came under French rule in 1839. They have been autonomous republics and members of the French community since 1960. The average temperature is about eighty degrees.

109

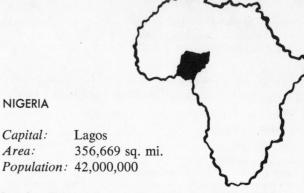

Stevedores (above) unload cargo at Atlantic terminal docks at Apapa, Lagos, Nigeria. Train (above, right) runs from center of Nigeria to Moslem north in Kano. A 25-story skyscraper (below) rises in Lagos, Nigerian capital. Pictured below, right, Prime Minister Sir Abubakar Tafawa Balewa.

NIGERIA

Capital: Lagos
Area: 356,669 sq. mi.
Population: 42,000,000

Leader: Prime Minister Sir Abubakar Tafawa Balewa

Nigeria is the most heavily populated nation in Africa and one of the most literate. She gained her independence in 1960 after being a British colony from about 1903, when a series of expeditions reduced the various district rulers to puppet kings under the British. Nigeria has cotton, cocoa, peanuts, palm kernels and palm oil as key agricultural products. Over ten per cent of the world's tin is mined here. Coal, gold, iron and lead have also been mined in some measure for years. Annual rainfall is seventy-seven inches.

Nigeria is the home of the Benin and Ife peoples, whose sculptures have been found in great number from a much earlier period. Like some of her neighboring countries, Nigeria has a great Moslem population in the north. Certain Nigerian groups are derived from pre-Christianity Hebrews who made their way west. She is a member of the British Commonwealth.

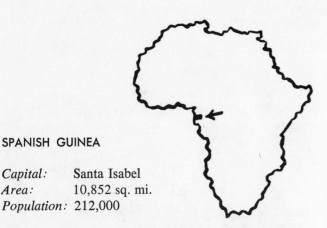

SPANISH GUINEA

Capital: Santa Isabel
Area: 10,852 sq. mi.
Population: 212,000

Spanish Guinea, including *Rio Muni* and *Fernando Po,* have very little commerce except in timber and palm oil. These possessions came to Spain about 1778. Rio Muni, like Cameroon, has a great variety of wild life including elephants, hippopotami, rhinoceri, gorillas and chimpanzees.

Left to right, bottom of page: *Presidents Moktar Ould Daddah, Modibo Keita, Hamani Diori and Maurice Yameogo.*

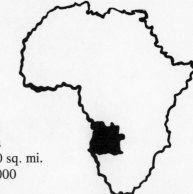

ANGOLA

Capital: Luanda
Area: 481,350 sq. mi.
Population: 5,000,000

Angola and the infamous slave port, *Cabinda,* came to the Portuguese as early as 1482. The land, more than ten times the size of Portugal, was consolidated and colonized three years later. The country is firmly ruled by more than a dozen governors assigned to a district. Recent riots and killings have marked this Portuguese possession. Severely oppressed, the Africans in Angola produce coffee, sisal, cotton, maize, sugar, peanuts, palm products and rice. Diamonds, lignite and copper are mined. Whale and other fish oils are derived from the fisheries along the coast. Livestock and wild game are plentiful. On the Benguela plateau the climate is good but below this tableland, which rises from 4,000 to 6,000 feet, it becomes hot and damp.

MAURITANIA (1)

Capital: Nouakchott
Area: 419,000 sq. mi.
Population: 727,000

Leader: President Moktar Ould Daddah

MALI (2)

Capital: Bamako
Area: 945,000 sq. mi.
Population: 4,100,000

Leader: President Modibo Keita

NIGER (3)

Capital: Niamey
Area: 450,000 sq.mi.
Population: 2,870,000

Leader: President Hamani Diori

UPPER VOLTA (4)

Capital: Ouagadougou
Area: 113,000 sq. mi.
Population: 3,635,000

Leader: President Maurice Yameogo

United Nations

Mission Permanente de Haute-Volta Apres des Nations Unies

Sketch at left depicts a musician and his stringed instrument. Below are the gray parrot and chimpanzee, natives of the Mauritania, Mali, Niger and Upper Volta regions.

Mauritania, Mali (formerly Sudan), *Niger* and *Upper Volta* were once, along with Dahomey, Guinea, Ivory Coast and Senegal, the territory of French West Africa. Mauritania is desert. Camels, horses, sheep and goats are raised by the people who live mostly in tents. Iron, copper and petroleum are resources which have not yet been fully developed. The only seaport is Port Etienne. Mali is landlocked and like Mauritania is mostly desert. No industry, it exports peanuts, rice and cotton. Niger's northern section is desert. Only 18,000 of its nearly three million people are wage earners. Its chief assets are peanuts, livestock, millet, beans and manioc. Upper Volta's main export is livestock. Her per capita income of $40 which seems low is standard for interior agricultural countries in Africa.

In these four countries which have continued as members of the French community since 1960, Tuareg, Moor, Arab and Fulani merge with Mandingo, Susu, Tukulor, Mossi, Dahomey and a hundred other people and languages. The Niger River prevents this region from being completely useless.

Tobacco farmer rides to market in Niger (above). Below, President Tshombe (left) of Katanga Province and Premier Cyrille Adoula of Central Government of the Congo confer.

Central Africa

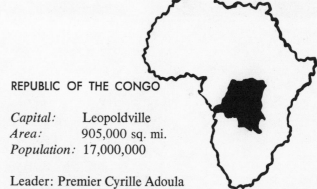

REPUBLIC OF THE CONGO

Capital: Leopoldville
Area: 905,000 sq. mi.
Population: 17,000,000

Leader: Premier Cyrille Adoula

United Nations

Republic of the Congo (Leopoldville) came under the personal ownership of Belgium's King Leopold II after Stanley discovered the mouth of the Congo River in 1877. Stanley was unable to interest Queen Victoria in the area, which is seventy-seven times larger than Belgium itself. Fifty-three per cent of her foreign trade is with Belgium. The great Congo forest, the Crystal Mountains in the west and the Mountains of the Moon in the east, along with the

113

Republic of the Congo Information Bureau

Congo River make up the most striking features of this great region. On the Katanga Plateau the mean temperature is about sixty-eight degrees and the rainfall around fifty-five inches annually. In Katanga province there are copper mines and the uranium deposits are called the greatest in the world. Congo also has diamonds, cobalt, gold, zinc, tin and cassiterite. Her exports include palm oil, bananas, cotton and coffee. The population, in this nearly bankrupt country, is almost totally illiterate.

When the Republic of the Congo was born June 30, 1960, Patrice Lumumba, 34, became premier.

Republic of the Congo Information Bureau

His assassination months later in the strife which afflicted the new nation aroused protest and concern for it was clear that forces outside the African continent were still interested in the wealth of the country. Lumumba would not condescend and lost his life in the ensuing power struggle in which were involved Congo officials, Moise Tshombe and Joseph Kasa-Vubu. Dag Hammarskjold, Secretary General of the United Nations, died when his plane crashed while on a mission to secure peace in the Congo's Katanga province.

On opposite page (top) are views of Boulevard Albert, the main street in Leopoldville and (bottom) Union Miniere du Haut-Katanga, a copper smelting plant in Elisabethville. At left is a Muluba dancer in Kabondo region. A helicopter sprays for mosquitoes and flies in Congo city above and, below, a view of Luluabourg, capital of Kasai Province.

Republic of the Congo Information Bureau

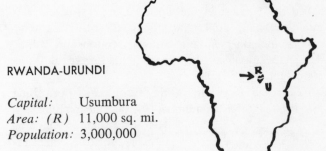

RWANDA-URUNDI

Capital: Usumbura
Area: (R) 11,000 sq. mi.
Population: 3,000,000

Leader: President Gregoire Kayibanda

Area: (U) 10,000 sq. mi.
Population: 2,500,000

Leader: King Mwami Mwambutsa IV

Rwanda-Urundi, a United Nations trust territory under Belgian supervision, was a German colony mandated to Belgium by the League of Nations in 1925. Lying in a belt of extinct volcanoes (Niragongo 10,200 ft., Nyamlagira 10,000 ft. are the highest), Rwanda serves mainly as a reservoir for the labor which works the Katanga mines. Livestock is the main product here, although some coffee and cotton are grown and some tin and gold are mined. Lake Kivu, 5,000 feet above sea level and fifty-five miles long and thirty miles wide, is said to be the loveliest lake in Africa. Wildlife, particularly gorilla, is plentiful in Rwanda.

The territories became with independence in mid-1962 the Republic of Rwanda and the Kingdom of Urundi.

Gregoire Kayibanda, president of Rwanda, and Mwambutsa IV, Mwami of Urundi, are pictured above. At left, top to bottom, Usumbura, former capital of Rwanda-Urundi under the Belgians, the sister of the Mwami of Urundi and Huro dancers marking the coming of independence to Rwanda.

King Rudahigwa (left), chief of his Watusi tribe, Queen Mother Nyramavuga (below), and a dancer (below, left), like most of the Watusi, average seven feet in height.

UGANDA

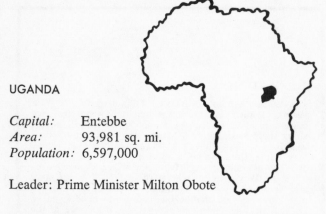

Capital: Entebbe
Area: 93,981 sq. mi.
Population: 6,597,000

Leader: Prime Minister Milton Obote

Uganda is directly adjacent to the northeast portion of the Republic of the Congo. The king of Buganda, one of Uganda's four provinces, is able to trace his family back to the fifteenth century. Protestant, Catholic and Islamic faiths collided here late in the nineteenth century and it took the British, who had protected it since 1894, about ten years to re-establish order. As if this were not enough, an epidemic of sleeping sickness broke out and lasted from 1900 to 1908, killing 250,000 people. Cotton, coffee, tea, sugar and rubber are grown in great quantities. Her mineral deposits have not really been exploited, though copper, tantalum, gold and tin have been found. Great varieties of wildlife include the rare white rhinoceros and five-horned giraffe. Uganda became independent in October, 1962.

Uganda Department of Information

Mercaldo Archives

Seen at left is Prime Minister Apollo Milton Obote, the Uganda leader. The crested eagle (below) and the striped hyena (bottom, left) are among Uganda's wildlife. Wazaramo couple (above) were sketched early in the 20th century.

118

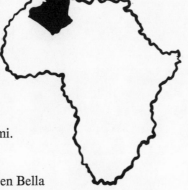

ALGERIA

Capital: Algiers
Area: 851,078 sq. mi.
Population: 10,000,000

Leader: Premier Ahmed Ben Bella

North Africa

Algeria is four times the size of France from whom she separated in 1962, voting for independence. France took the country with difficulty in 1830. Known in ancient times as Numidia, Algeria like most North African countries was a Roman colony. Pirates and slavers in the sixteenth and seventeenth centuries, Algerian sailors once raided Baltimore, Ireland, and carried two shiploads of women and children to Algeria as slaves. The United States fought piracy here from 1801 to 1805.

Although the French made certain concessions to the Algerian people, nothing short of independence halted the long war between the French army and the National Liberation Front of Algeria. There was a great loss of life on both sides and a vast expenditure of money. In addition, the war in Algeria severely

Top photo shows newly elected Premier Ahmed Ben Bella. Algerian farmers (above) harvest an important date crop.

119

threatened the political and social structure of France herself.

Petroleum products, machinery and apparatus including cars are produced in Algeria. Her principal crops are wheat, barley and oats. Tobacco, corn, flax, silk, figs and dates are also grown, along with wine and olive oil. There is cattle, sheep, goat and camel raising. Among her minerals, phosphates are numerous; zinc, lead, copper, salt and coal are also mined. There is varied wildlife. Temperature in the summer averages seventy-seven degrees; in winter, fifty-two. The changes however are rapid, going from extreme heat to extreme cold in a matter of hours.

The Beni-Bahdel dam (top) is one of many which aids irrigation of this arid Algerian country. View of Oran (left) shows the construction boom which arose from the growing and shifting population. Trucks and cars on assembly line (below) are being made in Algiers more cheaply than in France. The economy of such agricultural countries as Algiers is becoming diversified by industrialization.

LIBYA

Capitals:	Tripoli (winter)
	Bengasi (summer)
Area:	679,360 sq. mi.
Population:	1,400,000

Leader: Idris I

Libya is an hereditary kingdom and was until 1911 a part of the Ottoman Empire. In that year, during a war between Italy and Turkey, Italian troops occupied the country and won eventual sovereignty in 1912. The United Nations General Assembly voted in 1949 for Libyan independence which became official on December 24, 1951. The nation has a parliament made up of senators and representatives. Most Libyans live in the regions of Tripolitania or Cyrenaica; others in the Libyan desert. Cattle, sheep, camels and goats are raised in great number. Sponges and tuna fish are taken from the sea. On a small scale there has been some development of minerals: phosphates, manganese, alum, sulphur, lignite and salt. The hyena, fox and civet cat are common in Libya.

In contrast to this ancient Roman theatre at Leptis Magna, Libya (top) only one of many throughout North Africa, is this view of historically prominent Benghasi (above), summer capital of Libya, showing Roman Catholic cathedral.

The Arab World

TUNISIA

Capital: Tunis
Area: 48,332 sq. mi.
Population: 3,500,000

Leader: President Habib Bourguiba

Tunisia, a republic lying north of Libya and between Libya and Algeria, is the home of ancient Carthage. She became a French protectorate in 1881. Like Libya,

Tunisia was a battleground during World War II in the early '40s. She was granted autonomy by the French in 1955 and a year later her independence. Chief industry is agriculture. Wheat, barley, oats, sorghum, corn, peas and beans are grown. Cape Bon is the citrus fruit region. Raising livestock is also an important industry; there are over three million sheep here. Numerous cattle, goat and camels are herded as well. Iron ore, lead, zinc, mercury, manganese, copper and salt are her minerals.

Oil drilling such as that at Tripoli (left) is now commonplace in North Africa. The fennec (above) is a desert rat. Habib Bourguiba (below, left) is president. Kairoun is famous for its carpets and its Great Mosque (below).

The Arab World

The city of Tunis is also famous for her rugs (above, left) but not far away, in the sands of the country, lives the deadly horned viper (below) and the jumping mouse (above).

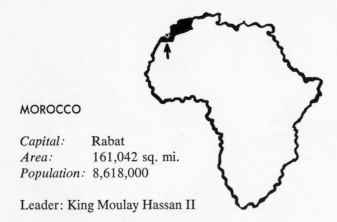

MOROCCO

Capital: Rabat
Area: 161,042 sq. mi.
Population: 8,618,000

Leader: King Moulay Hassan II

Morocco's chief cities are Casablanca and Rabat. Her minerals include phosphate (of which over three million tons are exported yearly), iron, coal, tin, cobalt, zinc and manganese. Though only twelve per cent of the total area is cultivated land, there are extensive olive, fig, date, orange and lemon orchards. Wheat, barley, millet and maize are her chief crops and the raising of sheep, goats, and cattle are very important. Morocco became independent of the French in 1956.

Above is Hassan II, king of Morocco. Kites (above, right) are scavenger birds of Africa. Irrigation tubes help reclaim arid lands (below). Right, a group of Moroccans; on opposite page, a view of the principal port, Casablanca.

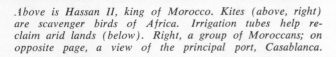

Minister of Information, Morocco

International Tuberculosis Campaign Photo

124

SPANISH MOROCCO

Capital: Tetuán
Area: 18,372 sq. mi.
Population: 1,340,000

Spanish Morocco is in the extreme northwestern point of the continent through which the rugged Rif mountains run. Rif tribesmen, led by Abd-el-Krim, almost destroyed the Spanish army in 1921. The largest city in Spanish Morocco is Melilla from which a large amount of iron ore is exported. Manganese, antimony, lead and zinc are also found although sheep and goat raising and fishing are two major occupations. Old castles built by various sultans can still be found. The city of Tangier is an international zone, although it lost this status for a time during World War II when the Spanish army invaded it. Its status was reinstated in 1945. *(Location on map is boxed area indicated by arrow on Morocco map, top, opposite page.)*

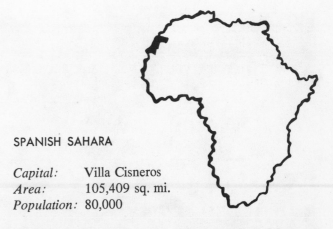

SPANISH SAHARA

Capital: Villa Cisneros
Area: 105,409 sq. mi.
Population: 80,000

Spanish Sahara is at the southern end of Morocco. Sometimes called Rio de Oro, this section is flat desert inhabited by nomads. Cod and shrimp fishing are done off the coast. Sheep, cattle and camel herding are prominent. The capital is located on the Rio de Oro Bay.

125

The Arab World

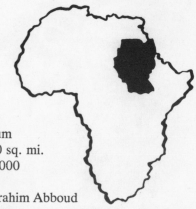

SUDAN

Capital: Khartoum
Area: 967,500 sq. mi.
Population: 12,100,000

Leader: President Ibrahim Abboud

Arab Review

Textiles (top) are prominent here; Sudanese (left, center) also ship 80% of world's gum arabic (right, center). Gold mining (above), along the Red Sea, is a growing industry.

Sudan is a republic which has been independent of the British and the Egyptians since January 1, 1956. Known in ancient times as Nubia, it is the country in which ancient Meroë was an important city around 600 B.C. The country came under joint rule in 1899 when British and Egyptian under Lord Kitchener all but wiped out the fanatical Mahadi who claimed to be descended from Mohammed and said they brought righteousness to all the world. They invariably came with the sword. The present Sudanese government is administered by a prime minister, his cabinet and a parliament made up of senators and representatives.

Cotton, corn, peanuts and oilseed are grown in the northern section. Salt is mined at Port Sudan, gold at Gebel Aulia on the Red Sea. Sudan also produces gum arabic. Most people raise livestock. Monkeys, lions, leopards, giraffe and ostrich are common in open country; elephant, crocodile and a variety of antelope can be found near the rivers. The annual rainfall is around forty inches and the temperature averages eighty-five degrees.

EGYPT

Capital: Cairo
Area: 386,198 sq. mi.
Population: 24,000,000

Leader: President Gamal Abdel Nasser

Egypt was declared an independent state by Britain in 1922, but retained the right to protect the Suez Canal. Though Egypt remained neutral during World War II the British fought at El Alamein to guard its canal interest. Gamal Abdel Nasser became president in 1956, heading a Council of the Nation where the power of government rests. Agriculture is the chief industry and engages more than half the population, which is most dense in the Nile Valley. The great Aswan and Gebel Aulia reservoirs provide the necessary irrigation for farming in the valley. Cotton is the chief crop; there is also sugar refining, rice, citrus fruit, soap, and perfume manufacturing. Wheat petroleum and iron ore are also important products. Syria, in 1962, dissolved her relationship with Egypt.

National Geographical Society

Flamingoes (above, left) live near Lake Mareotis, Alexandria. Cairo (above) is the capital city. St. George Coptic Christian Church (below) is one of Cairo's oldest. The historic gate (bottom) is to the Palace of Mex, Alexandria.

The Arab World

Small Islands of Africa

CANARY ISLANDS (1)

Capital: Las Palmas
Area: 2,807 sq. mi.
Population: 758,000

CAPE VERDE ISLANDS (2)

Capital: Praia
Area: 1,557 sq. mi.
Population: 166,000

SEYCHELLES (3)

Capital: Victoria
Area: 156 sq. mi.
Population: 35,000

MAURITIUS (4)

Capital: Port Louis
Area: 720 sq. mi.
Population: 420,000

The Canary Islands northwest of Africa belong to Spain. They are mountainous and largely volcanic with subtropical climate. Chief crops are bananas, tomatoes and potatoes. Mules are raised and exported.

The Cape Verde Islands due west of Mauritania on the west coast of Africa are a Portuguese oversea province. These islands which produce excellent coffee also export caster oil, sugar, oranges, mustard, tobacco and hides.

Mauritius Island and the *Seychelle Islands* are British colonies off the East African coast. Mauritius is of volcanic origin, with a history of severe epidemics and hurricanes. Its chief export is sugar. Seychelles is a group of ninety-two small islands in the Indian Ocean. Of granite surface, it exports phosphate, coconut oil, cinnamon, vanilla and patchouli.

Highlight Chronology concluded

1961 CHIEF ALBERT LUTHULI, LEADER OF THE OUTLAWED AFRICAN NATIONAL CONGRESS OF SOUTH AFRICA, BECAME FIRST AFRICAN, BLACK OR WHITE, TO WIN COVETED NOBEL PEACE PRIZE

1961 TANGANYIKA BECAME INDEPENDENT; THOUGH JULIUS NYERERE LEFT GOVERNMENT IN FAVOR OF PRESIDENT RASHIDI KAWAWA, HIS PRESTIGE REMAINED GREAT

1962 EUROPEAN COMMON MARKET ADMITTED MORE THAN A DOZEN NEW AFRICAN STATES

1962 AMERICAN PEACE CORPSMEN WENT TO SEVERAL AFRICAN NATIONS TO AID IN THEIR DEVELOPMENT

1962 NIGERIA PROVIDED TRACKING STATION FOR ORBITAL FLIGHT OF U. S. ASTRONAUT COL. JOHN GLENN

1962 PRESIDENT KWAME NKRUMAH OF GHANA ADDRESSED THE ACCRA ASSEMBLY; "WORLD WITHOUT THE BOMB" WAS TOPIC

1962 ALGERIAN WAR WITH FRANCE ENDED; WITH THE VOTING FOR INDEPENDENCE, RIVAL FACTIONS OF PREMIER BEN KHEDDA AND REVOLUTIONARY AHMED BEN BELLA STRUGGLED FOR LEADERSHIP

1962 RWANDI AND URUNDI GRANTED INDEPENDENCE; TRIBAL WARFARE THREATENED THE PEACEFUL TRANSITION FROM COLONIES TO FREE NATIONS

1962 FIRST MISSILES APPEARED ON THE AFRICAN CONTINENT AS A PART OF THE EGYPTIAN WAR ARSENAL

1962 CONGO (LEOPOLDVILLE) AGREED TO ALLOW ANGOLAN REBELS TO TRAIN WITHIN ITS BOUNDARIES FOR A POSSIBLE OFFENSIVE AGAINST THE PORTUGUESE

1962 UGANDA GAINED INDEPENDENCE OCTOBER 9; KENYA AND ZANZIBAR SCHEDULED NEXT